April 1977.

CUE FOR MUSIC

CUE FOR MUSIC

AN AUTOBIOGRAPHY BY

ERNEST IRVING

WITH A PROLOGUE AND EPILOGUE BY

DEREK HUDSON

London

DENNIS DOBSON

© 1959 by Constance Colpus

First published in Great Britain in 1959
by Dobson Books Ltd : 80 Kensington Church Street : London W8
All rights reserved
Printed in Great Britain by
East Midland Printing Co. Ltd.
Bury St. Edmunds, Peterborough and elsewhere in the U.K.

CONTENTS

LIST OF ILLUSTRATIONS

PROLOGUE

By Derek Hudson

Ernest Irving, who died on October 24, 1953, aged 75, was one of the oustanding British theatre musicians of the twentieth century. His score for *The Two Bouquets* is sufficient evidence of his skill as an arranger and composer of stage music, although his talent in this respect was overshadowed by that of his friend Norman O'Neill. It was as a conductor of a band of theatre musicians (or, in his later days, of an orchestra recording film music) that he really excelled. His was the hand that held together such memorable and varied shows as *This Year of Grace, Lilac Time, The Land of Smiles, The Dubarry, Merrie England, The Immortal Hour,* and the many others that he mentions in this book. To control a theatrical production in which music plays an important part requires not only keen musicality but vitality, adaptability, presence of mind, and the gift of leadership. All these Irving possessed to an unusual degree.

But he was something more than an accomplished theatre musician. He also enjoyed the privilege—and this of course partly explains his success—of being known as "a character", a distinction as refreshing in these days of uniformity as it is rare. The Edwardian gusto that carried him irrepressibly through the anxieties of a new theatrical production was refined by an individual analytical mind of a turn that might be called "literary", a mind that enjoyed the precise placing of words. It could be said of him that he jingled in his pocket the coin of the classics rubbed smooth by daily life. (Sir Michael Balcon has told in *The Times* of Irving's reluctance to arrange music for a memorial service for a colleague, because it was proposed that the translation of a poem by Callimachus should be recited on that occasion; he objected to the behaviour of that ancient Greek.) In his youth a keen rock-climber, he remained to the end of his life an outstanding chess player, who alarmed C. B. Cochran and others by playing chess with members of his orchestra during actual performances in the theatre.

All this unconventionality and versatility, which was seasoned by much geniality and humour, did not make Irving a pattern of domesticity; but it did make him a friend whom his fellow musicians admired and are unlikely to forget. They will remember especially that, though his own musical life was lived in the theatre and the film studio, his heart lay in serious music, as his work for the Royal Philharmonic Society showed.

One of Irving's friends was Dr. Ralph Vaughan Williams, O.M., whose recollections of him (contributed to *Music and Letters* of January, 1954) are here reproduced by his kind permission:

> To my great sorrow I only got to know Ernest Irving late in life: and, both of us being very busy, our meetings were not frequent. But I got to know enough of him to discover his remarkable and original mind.
>
> I first became conscious of him many years ago at a Philharmonic supper at which he made a characteristic speech. I remember in particular one sentence: 'Many people', he said, 'ask, are you any relation to Sir Henry? To which I answer, my only connection with Sir Henry is that my name *is* Irving and his was *not*.'
>
> It was a long time after this before I again came into contact with him. I had already written some film music which he criticised adversely in an article; not indeed for its artistic quality, but for its special mission as film music. In spite of this, Irving asked me to write some music for Ealing Studios and when, under his guidance, I made a success of this he

literally went down on his knees and apologised for his former strictures.

I wish I could have made notes of his delightful and informing conversation; but luckily I have kept most of his letters, from which I should like to quote. First, a letter in verse on the subject of using a singing voice in the distance at the same time as dialogue was going on in the picture. Here is some of it:

'UNA VOX ET PRAETEREA NIHIL

I very much regret to state
your scheme for treating number 8
has pulled us up with quite a jerk
because we fear it will not work.

Miss Mabel Ritchie's off-stage tune,
besides annoying Miss Lejeune,
would cover, blur, confuse and fog
our most expensive dialogue.

Failure they meet, and ruin black,
who mix two voices in one track.
Choose then a horn or cello, which
have different timbres, weight and pitch.

You would not wish, with sirens' tones
to deafen fans of Odeōns
who, listening to Miss Ritchie's A,
would miss what Kathleen had to say.

The frequencies her voice employs
should be kept free from other noise;
your tune should be of different hue
and run below or soar the blue.

Forgive me, Maestro, if I seem
to hold the voice in small esteem;
its use, like oboes, trumpet, flute,
is when the characters are mute.'

Here is another message in verse, this time a telegram sent to me on my eighty-first birthday:

> *'How happy to be*
> *the fourth power of three*
> *to think, make and see*
> *in old euphony,*
> *no jarring atonal,*
> *no twelve-tone grimace,*
> *full diapasonal*
> *strong counterpoints bass.*
>
> Can't afford any more, if Ursula wants to sing it the tune is Hanover.'

In case readers should think that his letters were always frivolous, here is a quotation from a letter, written not indeed to me, except as a quotation. It is about my Sinfonia Antartica.

> 'I think some of the modernists forget that the human soul is involved in musical inspiration, though of course the human brain is useful in fashioning the concept . . . There is no doubt at all that all the main themes were composed *ad hoc* and inspired by the history of the expedition on which the film was strictly based. They spring from the deep wells of the composer's mind, from which he draws his ideas, so that . . . desolation is the same thing spiritually if expressed by the South Pole, the battlefield or the Elysian Fields. The relations between his musical forms are therefore very deep down, and may not produce any similarity in musical notes, but only a similar trend in musical thought.'

Here is one more quotation on the lighter side. I had done myself the honour to dedicate my Sinfonia Antartica to Irving, and I sent him the original full score, saying that I hoped it would not prove a white elephant. Here is his reply:

> 'Of course I shall be delighted to have the score. The objection to the original white elephant was, I believe, not its colour, but its appetite'.

The gay and enjoyable reminiscences that follow will recall Irving most vividly to those who knew him. We are lucky, in more senses than one, to have them, because they were written by a very sick man.

Irving had been in poor health for at least the last twenty years of his life. Latterly only his remarkable nervous energy and vitality had kept him going. But when he relinquished the post of musical director of the Ealing film studios in May, 1953, he did not for a moment contemplate a life of idleness. Though confined to bed, he devoted himself with determination to a comic operetta and to the writing of his memoirs.

As he grew gradually weaker, it seemed unlikely that he would be able to complete his book. But his courage, his exceptional memory and his clarity of mind served him to the last, and when the end came he left the book virtually as it stands and with only the final chapter unwritten.

I was in touch with him by correspondence in the last months of his life and promised to do anything that I could in the way of tidying up his typescript and seeing it through the Press, if that should prove necessary. He wrote to me:

> There is one thing upon which I am determined even if it all falls down. I do not want this book to be didactic and professorial. Re-arrange it as you wish but I am sure you will remember in doing so that I am, in spite of my imperfections of style, a meticulous chooser of words.

It would have been not only a foolish but a hopeless task, as I assured him, to try to make anything "didactic and professorial" out of what he had written! But in fact I have altered the typescript hardly at all, incorporating only a few small changes of revision and arrangement that I feel he would have accepted. He had originally planned to call it *Seven Ages of a Musician,* basing the title on his parody of Shakespeare which appears at the beginning. I did not think this a very effective title, and when I suggested *Cue for Music* he approved of the change.

I am very sorry that he did not live to see the publication of his book and to know that it had been enjoyed—as I am sure it will be—by many lovers of music, the theatre and the cinema. Entertaining as *Cue for Music* is, it has its serious side, and all that Irving wrote about the technical aspect of his work will be recognised as authoritative by practical musicians. I am most grateful to his secretary, Mrs. Doris Davison, for her help in checking dates and other details, and to Mr. W. Macqueen-Pope for some valuable information.

SEVEN AGES OF A MUSICIAN

First the infant
Strumming and tinkling on his toy piano,
And then Cantoris choirboy, decked with cassock
And newly-laundered surplice, hymnal and psalter
Confidently treble. Then the Tyro
Testing, half-furnished, his uncertain craft
In the cold, open world. Then a fighter
Strange tricks mastering by trials long and hard,
Learning about men, climbing all the hill-tops,
England and Scotland, Wales and France and Spain;
Music, musicians, mountains—Then in London,
Taking life now a little more seriously,
Meeting all the masters who make our modern music,
Humbly their wisdom, work and genius
Trying to foster. The sixth age shifts
Into the lean and slipper'd pantaloon,
With spectacles on nose and beard new-sprung,
His youthful wiles refurbished—servant now
To the kinema; all the orchestral players
Back him with zeal, remembering
His work for better music. Last scene of all
That ends this strange eventful history;
Sans teeth, but still plus eyes,
Plus wits—and—thank the Lord—plus friends.

E.I.

CHAPTER I

"Prodeegious" Infant

★

I WAS BORN on November 6th, 1877, in the reign of Queen Victoria, in an old house on the slopes of a hill rising to the south of the ancient Borough of Godalming, Surrey; first born of Ashley Irving and Emma Fenner his wife. And that is all you will find in this book about my domestic affairs, except in as far as they relate to music.

As I lay in bed I looked between my toes to the distant summits of Pitch Hill and Leith Hill. Below my window, on the left, was a porch smothered with white jessamine; beyond it were lilies of the valley and a path flanked by rose bushes. On the right were sweet briar, a huge clump of lilac and a fertile filbert tree; at the far end of the garden were the remains of the village Pound, now, of course, fallen into desuetude and occupied by a huge elder tree, which, besides providing material for elderberry wine, was sought by all the youth of the countryside for the raw material for their pea-shooters, weapons very popular in that era.

On the evening before my birthday, this garden was the scene of an annual bonfire with a life-sized guy sitting on a tar barrel, attended by all the aforesaid youth in riotous enjoyment. The toiling gardeners who had to rectify their depredations took a dim view of this, but to me that evening, with the air full of the blaze and sound of crackers, squibs, catherine wheels and small rockets, was one wild whirl of exhilaration.

Beyond the Pound, from which the house took its name,

there was a little steep and narrow hill, with some steps at the top and wooden posts, from which I often surveyed the town in the early morning before anybody was up except me.

Godalming, which most people mispronounce, was then an ancient borough of 4,004 people. My mother used to tell me that I was number 4,005. It has a single, cobbled street, part of the Portsmouth Road, with many ancient houses; this divides at the southern end, and Church Street not unnaturally leads down to the church, dedicated to SS. Peter and Paul and possessing a tall, lead-covered steeple surmounted by the rooster of St. Peter. On the northern horizon could be seen the towers of Charterhouse School and the tall tower on the top of Frith Hill. Behind our lilac bushes was a field filled with artichokes, but I never saw anybody dig them up and often wondered what they were for. Behind the artichokes, Summerhouse Hill sloped up to the Recreation Ground, the path running through a wood which held a dark hole reputed to be a badger's holt and leading to Busridge Hall a mile away.

My grandfather, Thomas Fenner, very proud of being a lineal descendant of that Mayor of King's Lynn who thought up the idea of firing red-hot cannon balls through the Spanish Armada, was a fine musician. He was unpaid organist of Godalming Parish Church before they had a real built-up pipe organ and was, I am told, a first-class performer on the flute, for which he wrote many pieces of chamber music. He was also a magnificent calligraphist, and another of his altruistic activities was to write letters for illiterate villagers, who were more numerous than they are to-day. He died before I was born, and in my childhood most of the music in my life was provided by armies of song birds and by my mother's pretty little soprano voice piping a song beginning "At Five O'clock in the Morning". But when I was four years old I was taken every Sunday by my grandmother to the old parish church, where we sat right under the pulpit and the gaily painted decorative pipes of the organ.

My mother always declared that I was musical, and on the

Christmas Day after I reached the age of four she bought me a little toy piano with eight glass notes. Curiously enough, an uncle bought me a similar present, and somebody put one piano on top of the other and said, "Now then, Ernest, you have a two-manual organ." The Jubilate that day had been sung to the usual two-note chant by Dr. Crotch, and, thumping on the two-manual, I produced what sounded to my ring of admirers as the two notes which make up the tune. One of our guests who had a flair for fretwork sent me a set of pedals with metal notes, and another, I can only vaguely remember him as having worn a sword, sent me some dummy stops. So there I was, happy and conceited, with a full blown two-manual organ.

My father was not keen on this, but my mother, out of her pocket money, paid for lessons from the Town Clerk's sister, Miss Debenham, who lived in a delightful old house which might have been in Toledo. I was a very good reader for my age and a prodigious speller, having been encouraged by bonuses for lists of long words from my grandmother, who was very anxious to get me into the choir as soon as possible. I had a fairly good, tuneful little voice, but was depending on my power to read at sight.

So, at the age of seven, there I was in one of the six wicker chairs on the east side of the cantoris choir stalls, put there for the singing apprentices.

CHAPTER II

Cantoris

★

ON THE CANTORIS side ambitious choir boys had to pass the formidable obstacle of Smith, the Parish Clerk, a grey-bearded old gentleman with a loud bass voice and a thumb of iron which he applied behind the ear of any boys below him who chattered, fidgeted or otherwise misbehaved. Luckily for me, precedence in the choir was a matter of inches, and as I grew rapidly I soon passed out of the thumb's ambit and moved towards the top and underneath the altos.

There was great rivalry between the decani and cantoris which reached a climax in a fierce cricket match played at Frensham ponds, the scene of the annual choir outing. On one occasion I went in last with seventeen to get to win. I hit a full pitch on the leg stump into the pond, where the red ball bobbed about merrily. We had agreed there should be no "lost ball", but that everything should be run out, and the cantoris collected seventeen while the decani fetched a punt to retrieve the ball!

I was unable properly to boast of this exploit, because, after the match, in disposing of a jam puff and a bottle of ginger beer, I bit in half a wasp that had settled on the jam. He stung me on the tongue and I could not shut my mouth properly for a week.

The organist at that time was Dr. Edwin Webb, who had been at Calcutta Cathedral and who had brought over to this country as his wife Madame Alice Gomez, the famous mezzo-soprano singer. He spotted my liveliness in reading music, and it was soon arranged that I should go to his house for lessons on the organ and in harmony and counterpoint; clinking good lessons they were, too; I have never ceased to be grateful to him.

I used to copy all the new chants into the choir books and had to accompany Miss Gomez in her practising. I did not like this very much—neither, I imagine, did she—but in this way I got a nodding acquaintance with much popular music and most oratorios. Sixty years later, when my second daughter Echo was christened in Tarring Church, I found that the Vicar, Mr. Godber, had taken organ lessons from Webb in Calcutta.

Webb, somehow or other, misfired a little at Godalming. The choir boys disliked him because he put his finger into their mouths to see if they opened them wide enough; and he was inclined to be dictatorial with the men choristers who were possibly a bit old-fashioned in their ways. Before he left, I had my first professional engagement, five shillings for holding the keys of the organ down while the tuner did his work, and I was astonished to find that organ stops are divided into two ranks, sometimes quite a distance apart, each of which is tuned upon the whole tone scale. Before this, the shilling I received on Carpenter's Day or at weddings could be looked upon as a tip rather than a proper fee.

When Dr. Webb left he was followed by Mr. F. de G. English, a tall man with a blonde beard, who was a fine organ player, though he did indulge in too much Rheinberger and Sterndale Bennett. I used to pull out the stops for him and I remember he roared at me once in rage because I did not know that 'cello meant violoncello. He was a good cricketer and once when Godalming was playing at Milford I went with them as scorer. We were one short and I went in last, when English was 49 not out and we wanted 6 to win. I was hopelessly bowled middle stump by a slow straight good-length ball from the village blacksmith, and I have never been so ashamed in my life since, except when I gave a 2s 6d tip to a village rector, taking him for the verger.

Eventually English went to Halifax, and twenty years later I visited the town with a touring opera. I called on him and he welcomed me, but even over the hand-shake his pale blue eye took on a steely focus and I knew he was thinking of that summer evening under the spreading chestnut tree.

English was followed by a little Scot called Macintosh who, at choir practices, used to sing our part in a high falsetto voice. He once performed an oratorio in church with an orchestra and I was detailed to play the timpani and stationed half-way down the middle aisle. Some of my friends gathered in the adjacent pews and gave me such a hot time that I eventually came in a bar too soon with a resounding thwack. When I got back to the vestry Macintosh did not give me the pat on the back I thought I deserved but tweaked my ear in severe disapprobation.

CHAPTER III

Getting the Sack (First Time)

★

AN OLD LADYSMITH veteran who was in the choir with me turned up the other day and reminded me of what he called the Village Hampden Epic; how he found out about it I do not know.

A then well-known artist, Thackeray Turner, purchased the estate of Westbrook which extended for about half a mile on both sides of the river Wey. On the north side of the river was a sunken field bounded by a little brook and alongside this brook ran a footpath which was a short cut to the bathing house, free for general use when Charterhouse boys vacated it. Thackeray Turner put a high fence right round this field, obstructing the path and forcing bathers to make a semi-circular tour along the tow-path. I and another choir boy decided that this was oppression and we went one dark night, pulled up the fencing and threw it into the river. This not only freed the footpath but stopped the skin mill which was powered by a water wheel, so that all the workmen had half a day's holiday.

The painter came back with fortifications, a stout fence round the field and a concrete barricade over the brook just where a little box-hedged slope ran down from Peperharow Road to the footpath. We went to the village ironmonger and bought a tin of gunpower—for fireworks—enough to blow up the Tower of London, waited for a really dark night to lay our charge and a long train with which safely to ignite it. Then a terrible thing happened that made our hearts stop. At the top end of the little path appeared one of our three policemen passing along Peperharow Road. I suppose he smelt the powder, for he stopped, sniffed, and saw the spark of the train. Thank goodness he paused a few moments to decide what action he would take, for when he was half-way down the path the barrier went up. He might easily have been killed, but as it was his face was blackened and he was cut off from pursuit, so we safely joined in the crowd that ran out from the village to see what the noise was.

After this the artist took the matter really seriously, made the path completely inaccessible and started to grow grass for his hay crop; so having prepared an unassailable alibi by going to bed and getting out of the window, we went at the new moon with fishing rods and a spade, dug a hole through the embankment and let the river Wey into his field, which again stopped the mill and gave the men another half-day off. We were suspected but the alibi held. There was no gratitude from the villagers, as they now had to go farther round still, so we abandoned the rôles of Hampden and Cromwell, in high dudgeon.

It is true that this seems to have very little connection with music and I hope that after sixty years there are no Conservators alive to take vengeance.

I was designed for a school teacher or usher and had no liking whatever for the prospect. For the scholarship examination I did no real work, and I passed in the second class, which was of no use for a university career.

I was summoned to a meeting of the school board at the Vicarage one evening at 7 o'clock, but instead took out the punt and poled about under the bridge nearby. Most of the board passed over the bridge without seeing me, but the last one, a Mr. Daw, who was late and was hurrying to the Vicarage like the White Rabbit in *Alice in Wonderland*, spotted me in the punt and not unnaturally concluded that he need not hurry.

"Ernest," he called to me, "you are going to be late."

"No," I said, "I'm not, because I'm not going to go at all."

He reflected a moment as to whether he should "go at all" and then departed at a slower tempo. The next day my mother tearfully told me that I had got the sack and that the only thing left for me was to become the church organist. Having seen something of a church organist's life, this filled me with dismay, and as there was no family estate and I had to make some kind of a living, we sat in council to consider the future. Result—a blank: till one day in the Angel Hotel I met a man named King.

CHAPTER IV

I Emerge and find "Dry-ups"

★

KING HAD HEARD me accompany the singers at a cricket club concert and asked me why I did not take it up professionally. He produced a paper called *The Stage* (which is still going strong), showed me an advertisement in which a man named Johnson, at the Windsor Castle Hotel, Ventnor, was advertising for a music director for a concert party, and helped me to frame a letter applying for the post. I think it contained more lies than any one letter I have ever seen but I received a reply from the Windsor Castle Hotel asking me to report at once.

There was great objection to this at home, but I packed a bag, borrowed a fiver and set out down the Portsmouth line, over Spithead to Ryde, and then in the little yellow-engined train to Ventnor. Arrived at Ventnor, I asked a porter the way to the Windsor Castle. He cogitated a little while, unexpectedly, and then told me it was on the cliff, so up I trudged with my portmanteau looking for something that justified the title of the Windsor Castle.

I walked past it twice because it turned out to be a little beer-house by the roadside. In its window was a trough made by a sloping screen advertising somebody's ales, and at the bottom of the trough were the corpses of innumerable flies and wasps. This gave me pause, but eventually I walked into the bar (they kept open all day in those times) where the landlord was polishing up his bar engines, and asked for Mr. Johnson.

"He aint up yet," said he, jerking his thumb to the staircase, "first room on the left at the top of the stairs."

I mounted with sinking heart and knocked on the door. A deep bass voice called "Come in." It was a bedroom and in the bed was a very large negro who, as I entered, spat at and killed a bluebottle on the bedpost. Mr. Johnson told me that I started that afternoon on the beach, and that he should want me to play on a portable harmonium an accompaniment to the Toreador Song from *Carmen*, which he trusted I knew by heart, as my predecessor had taken the music away with him.

There were two other people in the troupe, one of whom, a nice man, was a clown called Schafer. I managed the Toreador Song all right, but got really scared when I was asked to go round collecting the pennies, or "bottle" as they called it. I thought I might easily find somebody in the audience from home—and that frightened me to death. I refused point blank to do it, which made me unpopular at once.

Ventnor being unprofitable, I was told that the next day we should perform at Shanklin and that I had to haul the harmonium through Bonchurch Chine. This beautiful place was quite lost on me. There was a stile in the middle of it, and none of my colleagues would help with the harmonium, so that I had to bribe a villager to give me a lift. After the concert at Shanklin I received 1s 2d, spending it on beer and bread and cheese.

I soon decided that my first essay was a washout. I went back to Ventnor, paid my bill, sent the portmanteau by passengers-luggage-in-advance, walked across the island to Ryde, took the ferry to Portsmouth, got the station-master at Portsmouth Harbour to telephone to the Godalming station-master to arrange for a ticket to be issued to me on tick, and arrived home defeated and downcast.

I sought out King and we searched *The Stage* again. This time we found an advertisement from Walter Osborne, the well-known baritone singer, who wanted a musical director for

Villiano the Vicious—this week, Town Hall, Sunningdale, next week Theatre Royal, Maidenhead. I wrote immediately and got the job, set out for Sunningdale, and made myself known to the company, which included a very good old comedian, Matt Robson, whose song went—

"Still his whiskers grew,
Still his whiskers grew,
He shaved them off,
He cut them off,
He mowed them off,
And he tore them off,
But still his whiskers grew,
Still his whiskers grew,
They covered the ground for miles around,
And still his whiskers grew."

The second boy and girl were two sisters, one a virago with a tearing soprano voice and the other a nice girl, a contralto with a slight squint. They sang a duet "Juanita" which I afterwards used in *The Two Bouquets*.

On the second week of this tour of 1895 we went to Maidenhead—the Grand Theatre, Maidenhead—an epoch-making day for me since I had an orchestra to conduct professionally. It consisted of the legal minimum number of four violins, double bass, cornet and drummer. They were not really professionals but tradesmen who used their evenings in this way to augment their pocket-money. They could consequently only rehearse in the dinner hour. There was no time, of course, even to play the music through, but I thoroughly enjoyed it, waving my newly-purchased baton in one hand and vamping on the piano with the other. Whether anyone else enjoyed it, I do not know. Not many could have done so because the large theatre was practically empty, and there was great difficulty in raising the railway fares to take the company to the next town, which was fittingly called Gravesend. Here the venture collapsed; the company disbanded and we were left with the familiar problem "Where do we go from here?"

One of the two "sisters" in *Villiano the Vicious* was married to a man with a wooden leg, named, curiously enough, Frank Swift. He was by way of being a poet and composer, and had written and printed an Irish ballad, which he used to sell from door to door. He let me have a couple of dozen copies at four-pence each, and my friend Lahee, who had been juvenile lead, and I started to explore the hinterlands of Essex, he to talk and I to play if necessary.

We found this a very tough job, and on one occasion walked three miles to see a musical farmer, of whom the local pub gave us great hopes. We had to wait three hours until he got back from market, and then he put the dog on us. This was a real discouragement, and we were sitting glumly in the churchyard of a place called Grays, when the Parson came up and talked to us. What is more, he bought a couple of copies of the song, though I think he could only have used them for jam covers; and, having wormed a little history out of me, he told us to call next day. When I turned up, I found my guardian there; he took me by the ear back to Godalming, and paid Lahee's fare to Croydon. Another melancholy failure—but it led later on, as failures so often do, to progress in another direction.

For the next "dry-up" I was engaged by a distinguished couple who described themselves as the Honourable Claude and "Lady" Gypsy Curnez. I opened at Bedford County Hall, and was disgusted to find that I was expected to assist in erecting the "fit-up". I refused point-blank, which did not make for my popularity in the company. Nevertheless, I was very useful, as, in addition to playing the piano, I played small parts in the repertory of Irish plays, which gave me more pleasure, I think, than it did the very small audiences.

"Lady" Gypsy travelled three hacks in a horse box, and a maid. They stayed at the best hotels in the Midlands hunting country, and, I fear, omitted sometimes to pay their bills. When we reached Evesham, the local paper gave us a somewhat sarcastic notice, in which they printed "Lady" Curnez's title within inverted commas. Her Ladyship was furious, and ordered the Honourable Claude to go and horsewhip the Editor, so he started off in full Cottesmore rig, and asked me to accompany him. As I had no wish to finish up in jail, I waited at the front door while he climbed a flight of stairs and knocked at a door at the top. In about three minutes there was a terrific row, and Curnez came flying down the steps, collapsing in a heap on the doormat.

Of course I screamed with laughter, but, in trying to get him on his feet, I found he had broken his arm, so I called a policeman, got an ambulance, took him to hospital and reported to "Her Ladyship". All she said was, "Who on earth is going to play Archibald to-night?" (We were playing *East Lynne*.) It turned out that I was the only person who could learn the words in time—I always had a phenomenal memory—so on I went, having played the overture, to double Archibald Carlisle and a comic policeman.

It was a poor house, but deserved something better than that, and at the end of the first act, when I had collapsed saying "Heaven have mercy on this dishonoured house", there was a small riot. Disregarding the protests of "Lady" Gypsy I stepped round the front of the curtain and faced the booing. "Ladies and Gentlemen," I said, "I know I am not a good actor (hearty agreement) but I *am* a good pianist, and I will proceed to play a selection from any Gilbert and Sullivan opera that you may choose", knowing, of course, it was certain that someone would say *The Mikado*. "After that, I am going to continue with the part whether you like it or not, and shall expect a little sympathy for the difficult position in which we are placed." This bravado made an instantaneous success, and every line, right or wrong, was greeted with great applause. "Splendid," said Her Ladyship, "We will repeat *East Lynne* tomorrow night." "Not with me in the cast," I said, "these chaps will come back with potatoes, and anyway, I have got another job to start in Goole on Monday."

"Lady" Gypsy was not so easily beaten; she refused to give up my trunk, and went off with it to the next town, Cirencester, I think. I went to the Chief Constable, who turned out to be a Masonic friend of my father's; he lent me a bicycle, and we both rode twelve miles over to the junction where the company had an hour's wait. He forced them to disgorge, put me on the train for Goole, lent me the fare Masonically, and just as I was thanking him and saying goodbye, he cried "Holy Moses, how am I going to get these two bikes back to Evesham?"

Goole produced another "dry-up" manager, in the shape of a gentleman who advertised "Search the world so bright and fair, you'll only find one Harry Dare". He lasted three weeks and dried-up at Barnsley. He popped up again the following year, advertising for people under the name of Willie West, so I spent one shilling on my old friend *The Stage* and advertised "Search the world with care and zest, you'll only find one Willie West", and that frightened him out!

The next and last of the "dry-ups" was a gentleman who had adapted the play *Naval Engagements* as a musical comedy; the only fault being that he had no money and no music. I wrote the music and we opened at the Theatre Royal, Hereford, on Easter Monday to a house of £9 gross. A fortnight later *Naval Engagements* came to a conclusion at Llanelly. There were two Irish comedians in the cast, Murray and McMahon, one of whom afterwards became famous as "Mrs. Casey", and they went to see our impresario in his bedroom to try and extract their fares home to Liverpool. He was a nice man with a very pleasant baritone voice, well equipped with smart clothes, and in his bedroom were six or seven pairs of boots and shoes on their lasts. When the Irishmen found he had no money for the fares, they selected a pair of boots each, explaining that they would have to walk to Liverpool, which they did.

CHAPTER V

London and the Arts

★

At this precise moment, my one-legged composer from *Villiano the Vicious* had got hold of some capital and formed a company called "The Music and Arts Corporation". They had their headquarters in the Adelphi next to the Little Theatre, with the name "Music and Arts Corporation" over the top floor, which was my office.

This was glory indeed! The first thing I did was to write a serenade, and the next, to find a pub on the corner where I could get a cut from the joint, a fruit tart, a piece of cheese and a glass of beer for elevenpence. That evening I went to the Vienna Café in New Oxford Street, a famous resort of professional and semi-professional chess players. The Music and Arts Corporation seemed to be doing little to justify its somewhat flamboyant title, but it was exploiting a comedy written by one of the directors, called *The J.P.*, in which my newly written serenade went as the *leitmotif*. Then another job came along which extended me to the full.

A young German pianist was being introduced to the London concert platform by the Music and Arts Corporation, and I was detailed to polish up her playing before public appearance. As she played the piano very much better than I did, this was a formidable task, and I am afraid I somewhat let the Corporation down.

I spent all my pocket money on the gallery at the Opera, and at Lords and the Oval, and I repaired to the Vienna Café on Sundays. Occasionally I used to dive into Simpsons, where the admission fee of one shilling entitled you to a reasonably good cigar as well as a game of chess.

Among the professional players at the Vienna was a distinguished looking gentleman who played in a silk hat and always with the same opponent. One Sunday the seat opposite his was vacant, and I came up and offered him a game. "Certainly, sir," said he, "but I always play for a shilling stake, as I don't like people taking their moves back when I catch them in a trap." A shilling was a shilling in those days, but I put down my coin, and he produced his. He played an opening called the "Ruy Lopez" and I played a crackerjack reply called "Mortimer's Defence" which baits a trap with a pawn to win a knight. My opponent walked into both traps, and after about the thirtieth move, being in an impossible position, he flicked his shilling towards me, saying, "I wonder you had the impertinence to play that defence against me." Says I, "I do not know who you are, but I got a lot of fun with it, and though it is unsound, I find many people walk into the trap as you did." "Yes," said he, "I *am* Mortimer!" We played many games together; he was a silent man and a very good player.

The Music and Arts Corporation, with its capitalized property of one ballad and a serenade, slowly wilted, and the finger of Destiny pointed to the road again. I met a man who had refused a job, because of illness, to conduct a musical piece with the astonishing name of *Cissy*, and although this was not very good, nor over-lucrative, the management was, at any rate, solvent, and I got my salary regularly at the end of every week, and started on a new chapter.

CHAPTER VI

"Fit-ups" and Smalls

★

Cissy WAS AN extraordinary little piece. It was a melodrama with music, and in it Daly himself played a Tutor in cap and gown rejoicing in the name of "Titus Thomas, B.A.". It had no chorus and only nine in the cast, so that it could run at a small cost in the small theatres, and occasionally in a larger theatre in the summer or for some unexpected date, with profit. Daly sang a song in *Cissy* called "The Weeping Willow Tree", in which I had to get the wind instruments to imitate him in his gags, which sometimes proved difficult in the better class theatre, where the players thought such gambols beneath their dignity.

During the five years I spent running around with Daly and writing music for pantomime for various managers, I did an enormous lot of mountaineering, cricket and football, but I did find time to write the music for a comic opera which Daly produced at a wooden theatre in Huddersfield. It was a most resounding flop, and I somehow do not feel that the music helped it very much. Daly died, and, having been turned down medically for the South African war, I found myself conducting, for the first time, a play with a printed score, *The Dandy Fifth* written by George R. Sims (Dagonet of the *Referee*) with music by Clarence Corri.

During the siege of Ladysmith, we were playing at the Opera House, Cork, and the comedian had to sing a song called "A little British Army goes a damn long way". Some Irishman in the gallery shouted "And damn quick too!" and there was a riot which was repeated every evening at nine o'clock; we never actually finished the opera in Cork. I was discussing the affair with some of our assailants in the theatre hostelry, when somebody coshed me with a pewter pot. He came round in the morning to apologise, and to offer me a free mount with the Cork and Muskerry Hounds, with which we had great fun, but I learnt from this to keep my political opinions to myself when visiting Ireland!

I was now gathering some kind of reputation as a good practitioner with a small orchestra, and got jobs with several of the smaller better class companies. In the summer vacations, one kept alive by orchestrating for singers and musical acts, and for the Phonograph Company, who were then making records on cylinders for public sale. In those days we used eight or nine instruments only, nearly all wind, that blared into an enormous funnel with the singer; and the balancing of all this needed a high degree of technical skill, paid for at a correspondingly high rate of 7s 6d a time! In the summer I took myself to Brighton and lived on thirty shillings per week.

Brighton was a grand place then; free chess, free bathing before nine o'clock, free golf (on an improvised course upon the Downs) and a kind pianoforte dealer who lent his top room overlooking the sea, with two pianos for quartets and other chamber music. An old fiddle-maker named Tibbalds had a vast library of music, and two string-playing sons, and occasionally we used to make a special effort, rope in some wind players with the aid of a little free refreshment, and play a symphony. Those were glorious days, and I was able, in the company of musicians of similar tastes, to explore the whole of the South Downs from Hastings to Hayling Island at a most astonishingly small cost. I remember finding an excruciatingly malodorous brand of tobacco which was most useful in the practice of economy, because one or two whiffs at a time were quite sufficient.

When the mackerel came up into the bay, we used to go in and stand on the sea wall side of the nets, and, as the shining fish leapt out of the trawl, catch them like a fast snick through the slips. I may say here and now that there is no more delightful fish than a mackerel grilled on a charcoal fire, with a little butter and parsley and a large piece of bread; but the mackerel has got to be stiff and straight out of the Channel. Brighton, I hear, is not quite like that now, and it is certainly more expensive.

CHAPTER VII

Touring and Mountaineering

★

An engagement to conduct *Floradora*—which was first produced at the Lyric in 1899—in a tour of the "No 2" towns commenced a period of progress and comparative safety. We went to pleasant places and carried with us four or five musicians to help the local players out with Leslie Stuart's score. I used to spend all my spare time in long-distance walking and mountaineering, wheedling the business manager into giving us the railway fare instead of the tickets, and in this way made acquaintance with nearly all the summits in Great Britain, though there were still some in the north-west of Scotland which remained out of reach.

When you take an actor on to a mountain you are taking a risk; I shall always remember planning to take one up Snowdon on a Good Friday. Ernest Peirce (a practised hand) and I were persuaded to take our business manager, and we met by appointment at the inn at Bettws-y-Coed and walked to Pen-y-Pas. It had been a wintry Easter and the mountains were covered with snow. It snowed all day, in fact, and it was not until four in the afternoon that I allowed them to walk along the P-y-P track and have a look at the summit, strictly enjoining that they should do no climbing, which was just as well since the manager was wearing a pair of patent boots. He ridiculed our equipment of hob-nails and axes, and when we sat down for a smoke at the far end of the walk, started on his own up the steep path which leads to the Saddle.

Before we noticed him, he had got into a position from which it was difficult to get him down without a rope, and so Peirce and I thought it best to tie our braces together and haul him through the cornice at the top of the path, and make our way down by the railway track on the other side. We managed this without any lethal results, but once up, in the teeth of a gale in the fading afternoon, I was rather taken aback to find that the railway track was ten feet deep in snow, and only the top of the signal post was showing. As all climbers know, there is a big traverse on the south side of the mountain, below which is a precipice; this slope was covered with loose snow and our manager friend, refusing to make the climb back to the ridge to get round it, started off straight across in his patent leather boots. I thought of his wife and of his company, which I think was called *The Music Maids*, but the Devil looked after him, and he jeered us heartily as we made the traverse round the top of the slope. We eventually got down to the Victoria Hotel; he ran on in advance and was dipping into the second pint when we arrived. He then announced that he was too tired to walk any farther, so we hired a horse and trap which we had to push up the steeper parts of the paths of Llanberis to Pen-y-Pas. There they had been getting ready to send out a search party when they received my telephone message from the Victoria. The manager was indignantly surprised at the cool reception which his exploit received, and for years after this used to say that we were frightened of a mountain footpath and that he had to show us how to tackle a mountain.

I had another adventure on Crossfell, a Pennine peak, with another manager, Jack Swinburne, the brother of Mercia. We were playing at Darlington and I planned a trip to take him to see Cauldron Snout on Sunday. We were standing on the bridge, admiring the cataract, when an old schoolfellow of mine arrived who had tramped from Appleby by the Pennine Pass called High Cup Nick, which lies on the flank of Crossfell, something over 3,000 feet up. His description of the walk sounded so attractive that I persuaded Swinburne to attack it, and off we went following the track of Maize Beck. Near the summit, mist descended upon us and visibility was limited to about five feet.

The far side of Crossfell consists of a series of precipices, down one of which our track lay. I was not sure which it was, and could not persuade Jack to chance it. Deep down in the distance, we could hear the village church bell and the distant trickle of water. There we were, thickly enshrouded, with no apparent alternative to spending the night upon the bare mountain, and the knowledge of Moussorgsky's score did not help in any way. We were both in flannels with nothing to cover us except a rather worn map of Cumberland. We had eaten all our provisions, though I did have four cigars left, but Swinburne had a bag of gold representing the management's profits at Darlington, which proved a great embarrassment because he could not lie comfortably upon it, and dare not put it down in case it rolled out of sight. We eventually dug a little hole for it under a rock, marked by sticking my alpenstock in it, and prepared to face the night under the shelter of the map.

When the sun rose, the fog lifted, and we stiffly dug up our bag of gold, and made all speed down the path (the one I had selected overnight was the right one!). While grumbling to Jack, I managed to fall into the Beck and got wet through. When we got to Harbour Flatts, the farmhouse at the bottom of the cliff, the farmer was most surprised that we had spent the night in the open. We explained that there was fog and it was dangerous to move. He said "Nonsense, there was a little cloud on the Nick about sunset, but that is all, everything else was as clear as crystal." So that if we had descended another five feet, we should have been in the clear. The farmer gave us a bath and a lift on a horse to Appleby, and, when I offered payment, would not accept anything except a book of comic songs which we duly sent on to him.

We were due at Stockton-on-Tees at eleven o'clock for a band rehearsal, and we did not arrive until three p.m. I think Jack took a dim view of mountains after that.

One could go on telling stories of the "great friendly faces of the mountains"—the Derbyshire Peaks, Snowdonia, the Cumberland Fells, Ben Nevis, Skye, the Cairngorms, Suilven, and all that wealth of beauty north of the Caledonian Canal of which Scotsmen are so justifiably proud. I shall always be glad that my touring engagements gave me the opportunity of enriching my memory with so many delightful episodes in close waistcoat-button contact with the rocks of Great Britain.

CHAPTER VIII

Madrid and King Alfonso

★

In 1907 Howard Carr, whom I had met in Carlisle, recommended me to Leslie Moreton, who was running a musical comedy called *The Girl Behind the Counter*. I toured with it for some months. Moreton, in connection with Guyton Heath, then made an arrangement to take a light opera company to Madrid, and he offered me the musical directorship.

Spanish affairs were making the headlines then in the English papers, as Princess Ena of Battenberg had just been married to the King of Spain, and if everybody in England was not studying Spanish, everybody in Spain was learning English. I leapt at the chance of visiting Madrid, and proceeded as rapidly as possible to assimilate Hugo's *Teach Yourself Spanish*, also the scores of *The Geisha, A Greek Slave, The Circus Girl, The Runaway Girl, Miss Hook of Holland, San Toy*, and half-a-dozen other musical comedies.

We rehearsed for a month at the Old Vic, and sailed in April for Vigo, in the *Avon*.

In Vigo Bay, I went out alone in a boat for a swim, got into a tide current, and being unable to find the boat, had to turn upon my back and swim for shore. Naturally, not having my Hugo handbook with me, I landed into some complications, but the parish priest lent me a pair of knickerbockers, and telephoned to Vigo, which by land was twelve miles away and too long a walk for one to attempt in a pair of borrowed knickerbockers if the honour of England was to be sustained. Safely back in Vigo, I returned the knickerbockers to the kind priest (they are all like that in Spain) and proceeded to defeat the local champion in a little improvised chess match.

We were to play at the Téatro Comedia, and we had a contract for not less than eighteen players in the orchestra. When I arrived there was a terrific and noisy argument going on about the number in the orchestra, and Guyton Heath said to me: "Ernest, I am afraid we cannot get your eighteen—they just won't provide them in spite of the contract." My Spanish, while not very bright, was better than Heath's, and I found out that what they were saying was that, if we opened as an operetta company with so small an orchestra as eighteen, we were foredoomed to failure! The complement was raised to thirty-two, and we set local copyists—very good and very cheap—scribbling away at extra string parts.

The orchestra—composed mostly of players from the Opera, which was closed—was really excellent, and they rehearsed every afternoon, though not for long. There were terrific pauses between the numbers, but the rehearsals were always pleasant. If I got stuck with my Spanish, one of the violas spoke French, and so we got on very well, especially as everybody, including the audience, was trying to learn English.

We opened with *The Geisha*, which our English company had been playing off and on for three years in England, and the first performance was timed to start at 9.30 p.m. At that hour there was not a soul in the theatre and I had to rout the orchestra out and get them placed to play the Royal Anthem. When the King and Queen arrived, the audience swarmed in, and the performance started about ten o'clock.

They had made me a great throne, covered in crimson velvet, which I approached in regal fashion from the centre aisle of the theatre, everybody shaking hands with me and talking English as hard as they could. The stage hands nailed the scenery to the stage, so the intervals were about forty minutes each, during which, later on in the run, I played bridge, then a new game, in the anteroom of the Royal Box. We finished the first performance somewhere about 2 a.m.

The King came to the theatre two or three times a week, and one day invited the company to tea at the Royal Palace, just outside the city. He stopped the car in the Calle Mayor to point out the place where the bomb was thrown during the royal wedding procession. On returning from the Palace to the theatre, the King said, "I always travel in five red Renaults, so they never know which one I am in. Which one would you like to travel in?" I voted for number one; His Majesty said, "No, that is forbidden; that is the one that would collect the mines." Nothing untoward of that nature happened, though Mr. Hook of Holland, descending into the wine cellar during the play, was pounced upon by the Guardia Civile who swarmed all over the place when the King was present.

The Spaniards, to our great astonishment, did not like our performance of *The Geisha*, though it was a careful copy of the Daly's Theatre production. We found out why when a touring company visited Madrid with a repertory which included *Carmen*, *Faust* and other "Grand" operas, with *The Geisha* unbelievably sandwiched in between. So one Thursday (the night upon which we did not perform as we had two performances every Sunday), we went over to see our rivals. We were given a great welcome and seats in the front row of the stalls, but as the *vendadores* in the front of the theatre sold our seats, we were soon politely moved back three or four rows, and, when these seats too were sold, there was another retreat of five or six rows, until we began to wonder how good the business had to be before we were thrown out altogether.

We soon found out why our performance was not popular, as the Italian company played *The Geisha* in dead, serious earnest, with a very stout and loud soprano singing a counter melody to the Goldfish Song an octave too high from the roof of the house with tragic accents of despair on every face. I am afraid that we rather rudely showed some signs of merriment, and in the interval it was suggested that as we disapproved we should not return. Most of us took advantage of this chance to escape from what certainly seemed to me a ridiculous travesty.

The opera that was liked best was, I think, *Miss Hook of Holland*, in which we had a stage band of twelve players led by a huge, one-eyed Spaniard who was addressed as Signor Bombo. He complained that the band-master's beat was inaccurate but after a few hot words it was discovered he was referring to the stage band-master, Lieutenant van Vuyt, who couldn't really conduct at all. He agreed to follow my beat but insisted that I should give the words of command, "a le derecho" and "a la izquierda", etc., which I did with great glee. The final result was that when the curtain fell it cut off Signor Bombo and two of his friends, who remained furiously drumming in front of the curtain. The audience yelled with delight and I had to shout for the curtain to rise, march them back again, and repeat the business with the same result. This happened five or six times every evening and was expected by the audience as the standard business of the opera.

A similar kind of thing happened in *The Runaway Girl*. There was a baritone solo in the first scene which could be sung by either of two characters, and through a little lack of precision in stage management both the gentlemen entered from opposite sides of the stage during the introduction and sat upon logs of wood which were there. Seeing me look somewhat surprised, the singers stared at one another, rose, bowed to me and retired, leaving the stage empty. I stopped the orchestra and played the introduction again; this time nobody came on and Leslie Moreton, seeing there was some mishap, sent on the dancers—our regular prescription for a hold-up—who started their dance "In The Shadows", humming the tune for themselves. I got rid of them with a few hard words, called on one of the singers again, and plugged through the song which was received as a comic number with great joy, and had to be repeated with all the business at every performance. This was about the only serious number of ours that they liked at all, though they adored the dancing and the comic business. I remember that we had to send to Barcelona to get a man to play the tom-toms in *San Toy*, and also that they received *A Greek Slave* with great respect, except the Hayden Coffin number, which they couldn't bear. Whenever anything went really wrong, on came the dancers and soon the world was all smiles again.

The people in Madrid were very kind but I found the streets dirty and malodorous. A blind man could find his way home by the smells. My very first lodgings in the *Jacometrezo* were particularly unhygienic, and I accidentally discovered a perfectly horrible scheme of domestic uncleanness which drove me to make a rapid change.

I found, eventually, one of Cook's agents, an Irishman named Murphy who had married a Spanish lady and lived in part of an old ducal dwelling. My bedroom had a stone floor and the ceiling was thirty feet above it. From it hung a long electric flex, of which the origin was not discernible. When I got very hot at night I slept out on the window balcony; I was occasionally prodded through the slats by home-going revellers, but altogether it was a most agreeable change. There was one disadvantage—there was no bathroom, nor were any public baths available; so that I used occasionally to don my evening dress a little earlier than usual and call at a big hotel in the Puerto del Sol, give my coat and 5 pesetas to the commissionaire, go up to the first floor, ring the bell for the chamber-maid, give her 5 pesetas, and have a bath. I told this story at a cocktail party in Madrid; it caused some amusement, but there was one person at the party whose face remained serious. I discovered afterwards that he was the manager of the hotel, and that was the end of my ablutions there.

At the end of the run, there was a week's interval while we

waited for the *Avon* to come back from Rio de Janeiro and I decided to walk most of the way over the Sierras. It was a strenuous hike, but I enjoyed it thoroughly. It was rather like a tramp through the western part of Ireland, not very clean but very hospitable. The rain cut short my walk after about two hundred miles, and I may say that when it rains in Spain, it does rain. It came down in steel bars and the rebound splashed one's chin. I finished the journey by train and was nearly dry by the time the *Avon* reached Southampton.

CHAPTER IX

Edward German and a Double Bass Harmonic

★

RETURNED FROM MADRID, and having distributed various small pieces of smuggled Toledo-ware amongst my relations, my next job was the opera *Tom Jones*, Fielding's eighteenth-century romance set to music by Edward German, which Robert Courtneidge had produced at the Apollo in 1907. Leslie Moreton had acquired the No 2 touring rights of the opera. It was scored for an orchestra of forty, and we should have to play it with twelve to fifteen musicians. This meant, of course, that German's full score had to be condensed, adapted and mutilated, a painful and tediously complicated operation for which German's permission had to be obtained. He was a most precise and fastidious man and insisted that he should vet every alteration in his music, so I borrowed the full score and set to work.

After a month's hard labour the job was completed, not satisfactorily, because making something worse is never satisfactory, however carefully done. The music was sent to German and a week later I was summoned to the presence.

In Hill Street, Maida Vale, there is, or was, a gate in the wall that looks like the entrance to a convent. I found it locked, and after I had rung the bell, a maid crossed the lawn and asked me, through a little grille in the gate, my name and business. She closed the grille, went back from the gate over the lawn, came back with a large key, unlocked the gate, let me in, re-locked the gate, and steered me to a waiting-room in the corner of which was an upright piano with an enormous music desk, spattered with inkstains of all sizes, shapes and colours.

There I waited a quarter of an hour for German, who, I verily believe, was doing nothing at all in the room above me. When he did come down, I shall never forget that the first thing he did was to offer me a glass of port wine, and the second to praise very highly the murderous work I had done on his score, which he truly said showed evidence of careful study and unremitting pains.

Coming to business, he said that, though there were several suggestions he would like to make, there was only one oversight he had found. The rest of this anecdote will appeal mainly to musicians.

There was a chord at the end of one of the numbers for the woodwind which had as its bass, a horn note, piano. It would have been easy, but wrong, to cue this for a trumpet or a trombone, and all the rest of the available wind was in use in other parts of the chord.

German agreed about the brass, but said: "You cannot leave the note out, and I have looked through the strings and it is not there." I asked him to check up with me and he triumphantly showed me the bar's rest in the first and second violins, viola, and violoncello.

Then I said, "What about the double-bass?" And there it was played as a harmonic, somewhere near the bottom waistcoat-button of the player, where the sound was reasonably like that of the horn.

German was delighted; he gave me another glass of port, and that harmonic on the double-bass was to have a revolutionary effect upon my musical career, a new phase of which started from that point. German came down to the first performance at the Opera House, Tunbridge Wells, and again expressed his appreciation of the ingenuity of my contraption.

A year later, William Greet sent out on tour German's Savoy

opera, *Merrie England,* and the composer would not hear of anybody to conduct it except "the fellow who did *Tom Jones* so well". William Greet and Walter Passmore, therefore, went to Blackmore, the agent, who put a shilling advertisement in my old friend *The Stage* asking me to write and send my address, for which small service Mr. Blackmore was quite well repaid by the receipt of ten per cent of my earnings from the engagement.

My doings, by no means glorious, between *Tom Jones* and *Merrie England* are recounted in Chapter Ten, and in that interval, as you will see, I managed to get the sack twice.

There was no rearrangement of the score necessary for *Merrie England,* as we travelled nine players to make up local deficiencies.

The first thing to do was to engage the first-class chorus singers which the opera demanded, and I believe I gathered together the finest body of singers that has ever toured in this country. Now this is not so easy a task as it might seem, as good chorus singing is an art very imperfectly understood. In Yorkshire they have several choral societies that really study chorus-singing scientifically. The perfect chorister should not only be able to sing his or her own part in tune, and in time with the beat, but should be aware of the composer's intentions as well as the conductor's directions. Each individuality must be merged in a combined and intelligent effort to express the whole work, and not merely to sing one individual part in it, that is to say, a good voice, good training, intelligence and enthusiasm are needed.

Every man and woman in my chorus was a musician who understood what he or she was about, and even in Yorkshire, the home of choral singing, their work was recognized as superlative and held up—for instance, in Sheffield, famous for its choir—as a model of what a chorus should be. They were all enthusiasts, and when they had the whole score by heart, German came to hear it and found in it a complete satisfaction of his musical ideas.

There was one song with chorus, "O! Peaceful England", sung by Queen Elizabeth, which ended in a long diminuendo upon the word "smile", and he tried this over and over again to get the final pianissimo down to vanishing point. But as I had already reached the limit of audibility, I had recourse to a little trick. I said to my singers: "Make your voices softer and softer for two beats, finish singing on the end of my second beat as softly as you can manage, but keep your mouths open until I complete the third beat, and then shut them all together."

German came up to see the performance at the Grand Theatre, Leeds, and at the end of the show came on to the stage and praised us all in words which modesty forbids me to repeat. He said that the diminuendo at the end of the "O! Peaceful England" song was the finest he had ever heard, turned to me and slapped me on the back, saying: "But don't be satisfied with the finish; you can get it softer than that," and to the eternal honour of my singers, I hereby state that not one of them batted an eyelid!

He was a great little man was Edward German, and English light music lost with him one of its strongest pillars.

The last week of the tour of *Merrie England* was at the Coronet Theatre, Notting Hill Gate. The management, who usually paid salaries on Friday evening, put up a notice that, as this was the end of the tour, and in order to prevent any last night junketings, salaries would be paid after the performance on Saturday. I was furious about this and went to the treasury demanding that they should pay as usual, personally guaranteeing the performance. I called together my wonderful band of singers and said to them: "Now you are going to give me on Saturday night the best performance of the whole tour, and that means something pretty good." They did, with the curious result which now follows.

That Saturday night, of all nights, was chosen by Mr. George Edwardes to visit the theatre, with his musical adviser, Merlin Morgan. They had come to see our leading lady, but Edwardes noticed that she was wearing near-white gloves which had not been sent to be cleaned. He said, "I don't care how good her voice is; if she wears dirty gloves for any reason, she is no good to me, but I would like to see that conductor chap who seems to be producing some extraordinary effects from the chorus." He was quite right—they were giving me one hundred and twenty-five per cent.

Walter Passmore came down to the orchestra door, and said in that curiously funereal voice of his: "Ernest, Mr. George Edwardes is in the box and wants to see you." I thought he was pulling my leg, but when I found he was, for once in a way, serious, up the iron stairs I went and knocked at the door of the box. "Come in," said a friendly voice. I opened the box door and fell down three steps on to my knees. The great man tapped me on the shoulder and said, "Don't kneel," and that is how I first met George Edwardes, due, you will please note, to that harmonic on the double-bass.

CHAPTER X

On Getting the Sack (Second and Third Times)

★

AFTER THE CONCLUSION of the *Tom Jones* tour I did several odd jobs, the last of which was to conduct a very bad musical comedy called *The Lady Slavey* which dated from 1894. One of the male characters was the ex-officer of the Connaught Rangers, Captain Dick Saker; he was a great sportsman and we used to dash off with the beagles whenever there was a pack within reach. One evening we got landed with hounds in the dusk on Mottram Moor and had to wait for the Master and Whip to find us and take charge of the pack. We were late at the theatre and the management took rather a dim view of the escapade.

Shortly afterwards, we were playing in Halifax and I received a letter from a friend in London begging me to come up for a mid-week concert which he said was going to be historic and for which he had bought two seats at the Queen's Hall. It was the visit of Artur Nikisch, who was to conduct the London Symphony Orchestra in a Tchaikowsky programme, including the Violin Concerto and the Pathetic Symphony. The local conductor was a good musician and knew the play, but the management would not hear of giving me the night off. I decided to take a chance and went off after the show on Wednesday night by the night train, attended the orchestra rehearsals, and took my friend to dine at Verrey's before the concert.

Maud McCarthy was the violinist, and she broke a string in the finale. She had no reserve instrument, but half the first violins took up the solo part and finished the concerto triumphantly. Nikisch was disgusted and stamped off in a rage, but the audience cheered the orchestra to the echo.

The second part of the concert gave us a magnificent performance of the Sixth Symphony, which was then quite new; I have heard it many times but never a performance like that, which made it appear a much greater work than it really is. At the end of the concert people stood on the seats of the Queen's Hall and threw their hats away, cheering wildly; we went out into the night drunken with excitement and very nearly got killed by being run over by a hansom cab.

Early next morning, in sack-cloth and ashes, back to Halifax. The performance by the local conductor had been excellent, but nothing I could plead avoided my dismissal, and I must admit that I deserved it. Somehow or other I didn't mind very much, though I found some difficulty in getting congenial work.

One Saturday night, of all nights, I was dining at Simpson's when an old friend, also a musical director, came in and joined me. When he found I was looking for work, he told me of a strange man, with an office in Arundel Street, who wanted a conductor for an Irish opera, *Peggy Machree*, but I said, "He won't be there now—it's 9 o'clock." "Oh," he said, "he is, I've just left him. He turned me down." So, off I went and searched him out—a strange grey man with a curling moustache, named Charles Hamilton, who was the London agent for the American Shuberts, and, as I found out later, their liaison with Seymour Hicks. I told him I had come after the job and he looked at me for a moment and asked me if I thought I could do it. "Of course I can," I said, "or I shouldn't have asked for it." "All right," he replied, "I'll engage you upon a fortnight's notice on either side. The tour opens at Birkenhead on Monday."

Well, the tour did open at Birkenhead on Monday, but only

just. The theatre had been closed for re-decoration and a brand new orchestra engaged. They looked fine but they couldn't play. I had a tremendous struggle all through the week and on Saturday evening received my fortnight's notice as arranged. I went on with the company to the next town, Leeds, where there was quite a good orchestra at the Grand Theatre. My successor refused to accept my offer of assistance and I had the grim satisfaction of seeing him miss a cue on the Monday night which plunged the whole of the first act into confusion. Hamilton sacked him, too, on the Saturday, but would not re-engage me.

The third conductor was a friend of mine, J. M. Capel, who had written a best-seller ballad entitled, "Love, could I only tell thee how dear thou art to me". Its success was said to be due to the fact that on the word "dear" the singer dropped to a low 'A' and held it, *espressivo*, like Sarastro in *The Magic Flute*. Capel was a very nice fellow but not a very good conductor and I hung around hoping for another disaster.

No such opportunity occurred, but Hamilton wanted a new song for his leading lady, Claudia Lasell, and offered a prize of ten pounds to be competed for. I set to work immediately to write and compose a piece of appropriate tripe, entitled "All you want is a cottage in the country", and entered it under a pseudonym. There were about 48 other entrants, including Jack Capel, and a committee sat in judgment. Its chairman was the stage director, who was very hostile to me and had been instrumental in getting me sacked for the third time. Capel played the numbers through, and "The Cottage" was awarded first prize unanimously and with acclaim. There was, as you may suppose, some gnashing of teeth about this, but I still did not get my job back, though Hamilton began to feel, I think, that he had made a mistake.

I hunted him down in London and he engaged me to orchestrate and conduct a musical play founded upon Amy Woodforde Finden's *On Jhelum River*, at the Aldwych Theatre. It lasted two weeks exactly. A little later, he got hold of a German musical comedy called *Das Süsse Madel* in which to star his American singer, and set me to work to score it and write some new numbers. *The Sweet Girl* came to the Shaftesbury and failed.

When Hamilton died in hospital, I was at his bedside. His last words were to ask my pardon, and I told him there was nothing to pardon, that he had fully repaid any injury he had inflicted. He turned his face to the wall and died thanking me. My words were strictly true; for Hamilton introduced me to Ellaline Terriss and Seymour Hicks, and this turned a new page in my theatrical career which was to prove both pleasant and profitable.

CHAPTER XI

George Edwardes

★

WHEN I ROSE to my feet in the box at the Coronet, Edwardes said to me: "Those people on the stage seem to like working for you, and I don't seem to get conductors who are popular disciplinarians. Have you seen *The Dollar Princess*?" I said, "Yes, Mr. Edwardes, and like it very much."

Edwardes: "Would you like to work for me?"

Me: "Everybody likes to work for you, Mr. Edwardes."

Edwardes: "You go tomorrow morning at ten o'clock to see Charles Cannon at my office in Lisle Street and tell him you are to conduct *The Dollar Princess* with Emmy Wehlin and Mabel Russell, opening at Blackpool in August."

Said I, "Thank you very much," and left the box for the second act. Edwardes called after me, "Don't slack off now you've got a new job!"

As I passed across the stage I told the chorus that they had got me a new engagement and they all cheered vigorously. The second act was, if possible, more enthusiastically sung than the first. Once again, blessings on that double-bass harmonic!

To be with George Edwardes was the top notch of a touring professional. Great fuss was made of the company in every town they visited and the seats were nearly always sold out before they opened. Edwardes provided cabs at the railway station labelled with the names of the principal artistes to take them to their rooms, and every kind of invitation was showered upon them.

The companies were moved from town to town in special trains with first-class compartments and dining car, in which excellent meals were served free. He did not mind what money he spent, but inexorably demanded first-class results.

The 1910 tour of *The Dollar Princess* was a tremendous success and was followed by *The Girl in the Train*, a jolly little opera by the same composer, which played for six weeks at the Princes Theatre, Manchester, with a tremendously strong cast which included Phyllis Dare, Eric Thorne, Louie Pounds, George Gregory and several other well-known artistes.

I enjoyed this very much, but its memory is slightly tinged by a dismal recollection of having backed the winners of the Lincolnshire and Grand National double at 100 to 1 and omitting to post the letter!

Edwardes was a most extraordinary man, with wonderful charm of manner which turned everybody that he employed into his devoted slave. Stories of him are myriad, and indeed you could only describe the man by telling what he did. He bestrode the narrow London theatre world like a Colossus so far as light music went, with Daly's, the Gaiety, the Prince of Wales's, and the Empire under his control. His kindness and generosity were proverbial, though there was generally some little steel core to his benefactions which later on proved of advantage to him.

When *The Girl in the Train* was running in London in 1910, Huntley Wright, who was playing the Judge, went off for a holiday in Switzerland while his understudy played at the Vaudeville. The understudy broke his arm, and they had to call upon the second understudy, a well-known artiste and excellent comedian whose Christian name was Billy. He doubled the the two understudies of Huntley Wright and Teddy Payne at the Gaiety. Billy did not know a thing about the part and the Guv'nor—as we called Edwardes—came down to the Vaudeville Theatre where I was rehearsing, slapped me on the back, and said: "Now you drop all this nonsense and come up with me to Daly's Theatre." There I found Billy waiting in the rehearsal room, and the Guv'nor said: "Now this room is yours, and I want you to go on rehearsing day and night until he knows every word, because if we don't get him on tomorrow night, I shall take the play off."

So we set about it, and at 7.30 p.m. there arrived an enormous silver salver from the Waldorf Hotel, with a complete seven-course meal, including a roast pullet, a Porterhouse steak, two bottles of Veuve Clicquot and a carafe of Cordiale Médoc.

It took Billy two hours—and a half an hour's sleep—to dispose of this, but he was awake by 11 o'clock and we were hard at it working on "Gonda, Darling Little Gonda", when Edwardes came in to enquire if we had enjoyed our meal, and to see how we were getting on. He seemed more pleased than I was at the progress we had made, and departed with encouraging words, enjoining perseverance.

When the coast was thoroughly clear, we started to pack up, intending to resume in the morning, but to our great surprise I found the door had been locked upon us, and no amount of hammering produced any result. It was a prospect not to be envisaged of spending the night playing "Darling Little Gonda" to Billy, and so I gathered a bundle of tissue paper from the wardrobe baskets which half filled the room, and piled it into a pyre upon the floor of woodblocks. When the fireman passed on his rounds, I set the paper alight; the fireman unlocked the door and rushed in; and we rushed out!

There was a very heated argument with Curtis, the doorkeeper, who said he would most certainly get the sack when Mr. Edwardes came in the morning and found we had departed, and we had to give him our word of honour that we would be back at work by 9 a.m. at the latest.

I took Billy home to my rooms and put him on the sofa, shook him out again at 7 a.m., washed his face and got him back to Daly's Theatre at 8.55 a.m., to the great relief of Curtis.

At 9 o'clock the strains of "Darling Little Gonda" floated out upon the Lisle Street air and at 9.03 a.m. the Guv'nor walked in! He patted us on the backs and said: "Now that is what I call real enthusiasm; your breakfast will be served in a quarter of an hour"—and it was. I am perfectly certain that the Old Man was not deceived, but you will notice that he got us to work at nine a.m. anyway.

We continued with the cloying repetition, getting hoarser and hoarser, of "Darling Little Gonda", and Billy went on at the matinée at which he dried up all over the shop. He got through the first Act, because he could read it at his desk, but when he had to descend, in the second Act, he could not remember a single word. They wired for Huntley Wright to return, but it was too late to save the play.

There is another story of George Edwardes which always amused me; it is about a brother conductor, Thomas Tunbridge, who tried for years to get a Mus. Bac. degree at Oxford University, but was always defeated, not by the music, but by "smalls" which has to precede the musical degree. It was very difficult for a middle-aged man without a public school education to get over this hurdle, but eventually he managed it, and proudly engraved on his *carte de visite* "Mus. Bac. Oxon". He very much wanted it put upon the programme, but Garrett Tod, the manager, said: "No fear, when the audience buy the programmes, they are inside the theatre, and it does not make any difference if you are the Lord Chancellor!"

Tunbridge was sent to Glasgow that year, to conduct a season of *The Quaker Girl* with Louis Bradfield, and did it very well indeed. Edwardes went up to see *The Quaker Girl*, sent for Tunbridge to his box, and congratulated him heartily. Tunbridge said: "I am glad you are pleased, sir, because I want to ask a favour."

Edwardes (mournfully): "As soon as I tell a fellow he has done a good job, he wants more money."

Tunbridge: "But I don't want more money, Mr. Edwardes, I am quite satisfied with my salary. What I want is my Degree upon the programme."

Edwardes (with eyebrows up): "And you don't want a rise?"

Tunbridge (firmly): "No, sir."

Edwardes: "My boy, you can have your coat-of-arms on the daybill!"

Poor Tunbridge. He came into £90,000 on his father's death, bought a Rolls-Royce with some of it, and killed himself by running into a tree.

The end of my first engagement with George Edwardes was unfortunate. We were playing at Bristol the last week of the tour. I was very worried about domestic affairs, and I suppose irritable and quarrelsome. On the first night in Bristol, one of the violins irritated me very much by looking at the stage instead of the beat, and I told him that if he wanted to see the show, I would give him a ticket for Tuesday night; in the meantime he would oblige me by taking more notice of me.

When I left the orchestra at the end of the act, he buttonholed me very rudely, and when I threw him off, swung a blow at me which missed. I hit him on the jaw, a little too hard I am afraid, because he disappeared into the Star trap—which had been most improperly used for sanitary purposes by the orchestra—and when he was extricated, he was not only very damp, but had a broken jaw!

I wired to London to my friend Merlin Morgan, who came up and took my place for the rest of the week. But this incident prevented the continuance of my job with Edwardes.

The Guv'nor went away to Homburg for medical treatment; while he was there, war broke out, and he died before he could get back to this country. I doubt whether the Theatre will see his like again.

CHAPTER XII

M. and Y.: Managing for Myself

★

I DO NOT include the Bristol episode among the "sacks". I left of my own volition and afterwards resumed my engagement with Edwardes' successor, Robert Evett.

Conforming to my principle of stealing an advantage from reverses, I made up my mind to take only London engagements in future and got several small productions to conduct in town, including one for André Charlot, *Dédé,* where I met Gertrude Lawrence and Joseph Coyne again. Gertrude was a delight to work with, but Joe by no means such a sugar-plum; he could not really sing at all and had original ideas about rhythm. I was very wary of him, however, and survived the run, during which the Prince of Wales was a frequent visitor to the Garrick Theatre, but the intervals between jobs was too long, though I filled them in with scoring.

Tom B. Young, who was the manager of Edwardes' *Dollar Princess,* had entered into partnership with Robert Macdonald, a Scottish impresario from Dunoon, to supply the smaller towns of the British Isles with the successful London musical comedies, played by smaller companies and produced upon a lesser scale. One of these was *The Dairymaids,* an old Courtneidge success from the Shaftesbury. It was by now in the sere and yellow leaf, but Macdonald had stuck to it valiantly and exploited it with dour Scottish economy. It still paid its way in the "number three" towns.

I went round to see them and told them my tale. "Well,"

said Mac, "there is the old *Dairymaids* starting Christmas Day at Whitehaven, and the Lowlands for the New Year. Five pounds a week; not much I know, but I will hold it open until the last moment."

Nothing turned up in London, so I walked into their office in Lisle Street in the middle of December and shook hands on *The Dairymaids.* As I emerged from their door, I bumped into Austen Hurgon who said, "I have been hunting you all over London. I want you to conduct *Arms and the Girl* at the London Hippodrome, opening Christmas." Said I, "I am very sorry, but I have just accepted a tour of *The Dairymaids.*" "Good heavens," said Hurgon, and so-on and so-on. I thought it would be unlucky as well as unfair to go back on my word, and stuck to *The Dairymaids,* thus commencing a pleasant and prosperous connection with Macdonald and Young which put me on my feet again.

Each time I asked for a rise in salary, which was pretty often, they gave me something more to do, till in the finish I found myself general manager, stage manager, and musical director of *The Count of Luxembourg* when the war broke out in 1914.

We were playing at Clacton-on-Sea. The war had ruined business all over England and there was a moratorium on all bank balances, but the local manager at Clacton was a sportsman. He had given M. & Y. a cash guarantee for their share, and told me I could draw it when I liked, though the houses were empty. So on the Friday morning I got from him a large bag of sovereigns, paid the salaries, bought the railway tickets, and set off to London with the rest.

I found Mac and Young staring gloomily at one another over the office table. "It's no good coming to us for money," said Mac, "we can't get any." My reply was to roll a hundred shining golden sovereigns out of my bag on to the office table with a result which might fairly be described as electric, so far as electricity can be expected to affect a couple of Scots.

All touring companies had to be withdrawn and nearly all their dates were cancelled, but I obtained permission from M. & Y. to try to run the tour at my own risk. The company joyously agreed to work on shares, and I inserted a good British patriotic song into the middle of the second act. Those who remember the operetta will recollect that a really essential part of the scenery was the staircase up and down which the principals danced in the waltz number; so I got the carpenter to saw the stairs up and the gentlemen of the company carried a piece each in a canvas bag on the railway journey, when there were any trains available. Some of our theatres were occupied by troops, and then I took on dates that had been dropped by called-in companies. If our scenery did not get through, we used what we had. We were welcome everywhere and business was very good; good enough to pay the company a bonus over and above their original contract.

Things settled down a little and M. & Y. announced their intention of taking up the management again for themselves. "Look here," said Mac to me, "if you're so clever, there is *The Gay Gordons;* you could book a good tour in Scotland where you started with me in *The Dairymaids*. There is a Yorkshireman, who wants to put up some money, with whom you could go into partnership, but this would have to be off your own bat, and, meanwhile, will you please take out that patriotic song."

I met the Yorkshireman and made the partnership, but he never came along with the cash; and, having engaged and rehearsed the company, I was faced with the formidable task of finding the fares to Kirkcaldy, where I had booked the opening fortnight of the New Year. I forget how this was managed, some arrangement between the railway company and the Kirkcaldy manager, I expect. Maybe I had remembered one of "Lady" Gypsy's dodges, but we got to Fifeshire and opened to a tremendous house. Kirkcaldy turned up trumps and provided funds to finance the rest of the tour:— Perth, Kilmarnock,

Paisley, Greenock, Ayr, Stirling, Falkirk, Coatbridge, Motherwell and Dumfries—all proved paying engagements. I very nearly finished by enlisting into the "Gay Gordons" myself, but was kept out by a defective heart.

It was a very exciting adventure, but not one to be repeated, and back in London I was very glad to get an engagement to deputise for Howard Carr at the Empire.

CHAPTER XIII

Howard Carr and the Savage Club

★

It was in 1899 that I met Howard Carr, he tells me; though it seems impossible to me that it could have been so long ago. We met at Carlisle, where his uncle Howard Talbot, the famous musical comedy composer, had sent him to learn the job of a musical director at His Majesty's Theatre there. He had a little orchestra of about eight which he conducted in full evening dress with white kid gloves—a most impressive general for such a small army. When a travelling conductor visited his theatre, Carr would, and did, play any one of various instruments upon which he had attained various degrees of proficiency; horn, 'cello or timpani, the last mentioned being probably his best show.

We took to one another at once, and after the performance walked by the bank of the River Eden talking music and philosophy, returning to his rooms about two a.m. for a game of chess. I don't know what his landlady thought about it, mine thought we were mad. Carr duly got promotion, and years later I found him established in London as a conductor of musical comedy. During the first war he conducted *The Lilac Domino* at the Empire Theatre, and, finding that he required a month's holiday, engaged me to deputise for him, thus providing me with a very useful *entrée* to the London West-end theatres.

What is more, he proposed me for the Savage Club, where I met in social friendship many musicians who up till then had only been names or professional acquaintances; they included Norman O'Neill, Herman Finck, Philip Page and a whole lot of painters, actors, scientists and literary men whose friendship added four dimensions to life, and, incidentally, quite cured me of any desire to continue running round the provinces. The food was good as well as the company, and my weight rose beyond the point when one could stick safely on to the rocks of Scafell Pike with the aid of a good hairy waistcoat.

Carr was a very energetic worker for his brother musicians, as well as for himself. He formed an association of British conductors, with the excellent idea of keeping them independent of the managers they worked for and of the musicians they had to control, and he roped me in to help as treasurer. It seems to me obvious that in the case of trouble between theatre managers and their orchestral players the director should not be committed to either side; he has both managerial and musical responsibility. The Association prospered for some years, steering a perilous course between Scylla and Charybdis, but it weakened and eventually disappeared as cinemas and dance music flooded out the provincial orchestras.

Carr became the municipal music director for Harrogate and eventually went to Australia where he took the lead in theatrical music. Returning to this country, he found things entirely changed—with jazz and dance-band music where orchestras once played and American musical comedy standing triumphant over the corpse of English light opera. He still writes good stout dramatic music, but the world in which he was preeminent has passed away. As poor Jo said in *Bleak House*, "He wos wery good to me, he wos!" and his help and encouragement had a great effect in the fifth age of my seven.

CHAPTER XIV

Herman Finck and Paris

★

HERMAN FINCK was one of the most baffling personalities I ever met. He could be, and was, mean and benevolent, spiteful and sympathetic, jealous and generous, selfish and sociable. Of Dutch origin, he developed into the most metropolitan of Londoners, and when he followed Alfred Plumpton at the Palace, he soon became the most popular musical director of English light music. Sir Alfred Butt took over the Palace Theatre, and Finck wrote the music for the revue successes produced there, which included world-famous tunes such as "Gilbert the Filbert" and "In the Shadows". Then Sir Alfred assumed control of Drury Lane, and Herman moved over with his brass plate and settled down as music director of the national theatre. He did not much relish my invasion of the Palace Theatre with Seymour Hicks, and when Butt built the Palace (now the Mogador) in Paris, he offered me the post of music director, to open with a revue in which the star was Régine Flory, a French comedienne with whom Herman did not get on too well in London.

The Versailles Peace Conference was in full swing. Paris was crammed with Americans; President Woodrow Wilson came to the first night and attended frequently afterwards. One of the star items was a ballet in which M'selle Flory danced on water-lily leaves to Finck's music. The leaves were of cast-iron, but Flory had put on weight and the ballet lost its magic. She engaged a Frenchman to write the music for a very rude replacement called "Hercule au pieds d'Omphâle", which I innocently rehearsed and put into the programme, not dreaming that the substitution had received no sanction from headquarters.

The French pit and gallery loved the new opus; Finck came over and cursed; Butt came over and wept. We did pretty well while the Americans were around, but the French never really understood us, especially our comedians. French music directors seem to exist upon performing-right fees, and at that time their fixed salaries were about £8 a month. There was a grand inquisition into my contract by the French Musicians' Union to make certain that I was not undercutting the local talent, and the officials were considerably startled to find I was getting twenty times that amount. "Ah! Sir Butt!" said the senior shop steward, "Il est fou!"

All kinds of strange things happened during the season in Paris. I was once walking to rehearsal with Gwennie Brogden in a thunderstorm, and we found propped up against the pit entrance an American soldier very tight and very wet, apparently fast asleep. Gwennie enquired if there was anything we could do for him but with no response whatever. She went up to the soldier and tapped him on the shoulder; he slid slowly and silently down into a puddle at his feet. We yanked him up again and shouted in his ear, "We are English. Is there anything we can do to make you more comfortable?" He slowly opened one blue eye and fixed it gravely on the actress. "Well, lady," he ejaculated thickly, "you might jest have it stop rainin'," and sank smilingly back into his puddle.

The Parish Palace, as it was called, failed, and we all came back to London, where Finck gave me the most difficult job I have ever had in all my life, to conduct a variety programme at the Empire. Music in the variety halls was just changing over to the dance-band type and the principal qualifications needed by a successful music director were a flair for the on-coming jazz and a knowledge of the gags and business of the new type of comedian, none of which I possessed. I had a fine orchestra and a considerable amount of prestige, but I am sure that most of the turns considered us hopelessly high-brow and "old school tie". Straw-hatted Gillie Potter was one of our best friends, because he had no music at all except for the beginning and end of his turn, but even he had to be watched carefully. Whether or not he was paid for it by coin or barter, I do not know, but nine times in his "act" he used the words "Watney's Brewery", the ninth—or was it the eighth?—time being the cue for the curtain music. At matinées, I believe it was the seventh.

Having survived, not without some scars of battle, the variety season, I conducted at the Empire a musical comedy called *The Red Mill* in which Little Tich was the star, and though this turned out to be a failure, I was now on my way to establishing myself as a West-end conductor.

When *The Red Mill* ceased to turn, the Empire was let by Sir Alfred Butt to the Gaumont-British Film Producing Company for their trade-shows, and this led to my first venture into the world of celluloid. New films were shown to exhibitors at a London theatre, accompanied by orchestral music fitted more or less to the action, and the setting of one of these, *The Two Little Vagabonds,* was considered to be unsuitable. A lot of classical music, including Schubert's "Unfinished" Symphony, had been linked to the drama and weighed the comedy down. Sir Alfred had the idea that, having just returned from Paris, I might be able to find some tunes which would restore the gaiety of the French original, and, with the help of Maurice Chevalier and Mistinguette, I did so, the result being that I got several more films to set and became quite a "big shot" in this line of business.

I am sorry to confess that, later on, I too succumbed to the temptation to use good music, and was severely admonished by an exhibitor from Rawtensall who demanded angrily where he was to get musicians to play Richard Strauss's *Salome,* which I had used as the accompaniment to the film he had booked. We explained to him gently that the Strauss score was only used to sell *him* the film, and that we supplied with the picture a list of simpler music which could be used locally in its stead.

When talking-films came in, William J. Wilson, producer of *The Lilac Domino,* formed a small company and hired Professor Herkomer's studio at Bushey to make one. We were to start with opera, *Romeo and Juliet,* no less, with Desirée Ellinger in the chief part. I re-scored Gounod for a band of fourteen, and the synchronized sound, made behind a glass screen, was recorded on discs. We had all sorts of trouble and the players, underpaid, changed every day. The Musicians' Union posted a scout at the lane-end to warn their members off; of course, the result was a fiasco, but I found out quite a lot of things *not* to do when making a sound-film. During the work at Bushey, Mr. de Forest brought out and showed us what I believe was the first sound recorded on film; but by now Wilson had spent all his money.

Finck later on engaged me for *The Curate's Egg*—thus providing the opportunity for my fourth "sack"—and, what was better, he deserted *The Two Bouquets* for *The Desert Song,* which introduced me to the Farjeons, so that altogether I should be, and am, duly grateful. One queer thing I remember about him; although he made tons of money, he never bought a car but went everywhere in taxis. He gave as a reason, whether seriously or not I do not know, that if he left his car outside anybody's door, everybody would know that Finck was inside.

The English flower in the ~~German~~ Conservatory

Imaginary sketch of Norman O'Neill by Aubrey Beardsley, sent to O'Neill while studying in Frankfurt about 1893.

CHAPTER XV

Norman O'Neill

★

AFTER EDWARD GERMAN, Norman O'Neill was the man who had most influence upon my musical life. I first met this lovable Irishman at Howard Carr's "Conductors' Association" and when I joined the Savage Club in 1917 we soon became firm friends. At that time O'Neill was music director of the Haymarket Theatre, honorary treasurer of the Royal Philharmonic Society, and a member of the Savage Club committee. He was enormously popular and had friends all over the world; his incidental music, particularly that for *The Blue Bird* and *Mary Rose*, made him famous in the theatre world, and his work for the Philharmonic Society brought him into contact with all the great musicians of his day. He lived in an old house in Kensington; it had a lovely walled garden at the back, with a big studio where he could be undisturbed when composing or scoring. On Sunday evenings you could always find three or four musical notabilities in the drawing-room, discussing all kinds of musical topics or being entertained by his charming wife Adine, herself a fine musician and first-class pianist, a pupil of Madame Clara Schumann. There, among many others, I met Gustav Holst, Cyril Scott, Percy Grainger, Theodore Holland, and on one notable occasion—Frederick Delius.

Delius was a great friend of Norman, who used to visit him regularly at his home at Grez, in the forest of Fontainebleau. One day he brought Delius to the Savage Club. The great man arrived at Victoria with an enormous iron-clad trunk full of music; it weighed about 6 cwt. and the porters left it severely alone. At the club Delius remembered it, and would not settle down until something was done about it. No taxi would look at it, but eventually we got an ancient growler with a strong wooden roof, and with one of us at each end of the top deck, grabbing the ropes, we got it safely to Adelphi Terrace and plonked it down in the hall, where it made a considerable dent in the linoleum. Even then Delius would not keep quiet until seven dogs belonging to members, who had given the trunk an eager welcome, had been tied up out of range.

Every time I have met a great or good composer I have cross-examined him as to the working of inspiration in composition. I am not going to tell you what they said, but I am sure you would be astonished to know their wide range of difference. Painters, on the other hand, questioned as to which they considered the greatest painting in the world, voted—70%of them—solidly for one painting, El Greco's "Agony in the Garden".

Norman soon found ways of using my experience and practical approach to music, and quickly had me on the committee of the Savage and the "Phil"—of which more later. He also set me off conducting *Mary Rose, The Way of an Eagle, Julius Caesar* with Henry Ainley, and *Macbeth.*

The *Caesar* tour was fine fun, except that the Forum scene was so harrowing that I could not bear to sit it out twice a day. Claud Rains played Cassius and very fine he was, in spite of his lack of inches (vertical). Stanley Bell (who produced it) rehearsed a crowd of local extras every week, and one Sunday night at Sheffield Ainley and I looked in on him at the Lyceum. He was rehearsing Caesar's entrance and said "When the lictors raise their fasces, you all say 'Ave'." He then went off, re-entered and lifted his umbrella, closed, into the air. "Ave", muttered everybody, including Ainley and me. "Go away," said Stanley to us, fiercely.

On Monday evening I was playing Norman's entrance march

Caricature of Henry Ainley in *Julius Caesar* by J. H. Dowd, presented by Ainley to Norman O'Neill.

and the extras were kneeling all over the stage with their backs to the audience. On came the lictors, up went their fasces. Said the nearest steel-puddler to his neighbour, "This is where we say 'Arvey'." "Naw," was the rejoinder, "that ain't 'Arvey', wait for the bloke with the umbereller!"

When Norman was asked by J. K. Hackett to write music for *Macbeth* in 1920 he was delighted, and I was able to be of immediate service, in that I insisted he should double the fee he had intended to ask. Hackett never turned a hair—I think he would have re-doubled if pressed—and Norman started by writing the witch-music on the lines of *Mary Rose*, only this time the three voices in the orchestra pit were men. Their Ha! Ha! Ha!; Hee! Hee! Hee!; Ho! Ho! Ho! hardly came off, and was at times a bit too close to the comic vein, but there was plenty of other good music including some fine blood-boltered stuff for Banquo.

Hackett was a big slow man, bearded, rather like Chaliapin in the part. He was not a very good actor, but spoke Shakespeare's lines beautifully in a deep resonant bass which must have made some of our modern Macbeths jealous. In one scene he went down on the word "hell" to bottom D flat; it was so accurate and musical that I could have strengthened it with a bassoon note with safety. He brought with him from America some enormous scenery and built up a real Cawdor Castle on the stage of the Aldwych. The Cauldron Scene would only just go into the theatre, and had to be taken out and stored every night.

Mrs. Patrick Campbell was the Lady Macbeth and Louis Calvert, a bastion of the old School, was the producer; the rehearsals were as interesting as a test match. One of the earliest quarrels was about Mrs. Pat's nightgown for the sleep-walking scene. She wanted something glamorous and shiny. He produced a dingy replica of something Mrs. Siddons had worn. "It looks like dirty calico," she said. "It looks exactly right to me," said Calvert. "Oh," was the very impolite rejoinder, "you are probably used to dirty nightgowns."

Every time Norman entered the theatre she stopped the rehearsal and called to him to play her "peeebroch"— just once! and was continually missing when her entrance came. Once Calvert, a bulky man, was climbing up the steps over the orchestra pit to correct her in something—his head slowly rose above the floats—"Thus bad begins," declaimed Mrs. Pat, and, after the next wiggle, "and worse remains behind."

At last Calvert became so exasperated that he persuaded Hackett to promise that if Mrs. Pat absented herself without permission again he would re-cast the part. The very next day her entrance cue brought no response. "I expect," said J.K., "she has just gone up to the wardrobe." This, by the way, was on the fifth floor, near the roof of the theatre. A white-faced assistant stage-manager poked his nose in, despite heavy winks from his employer; "I don't think she's gone to the wardrobe, sir," he stammered. *"And why not?"* thundered Hackett. "Sh-sh-she went in a taxi, sir," replied the boy as he dodged J.K's toe-cap.

Somehow or other things were patched up and the show went on. At the last minute Calvert insisted on music (hurry-music he called it) through the Courtyard Scene after the murder. Everybody was shocked, even Mrs. Pat. In vain we protested that if ever there was a scene that needed no music, this was it; to keep him quiet Norman wrote a "hurry" and we played it at the dress-rehearsal to Calvert's great delight. After the rehearsal Norman came down into the pit, collected the band parts of the "hurry" and meticulously tore them into very small pieces, which he placed carefully in the dust-bin.

About a month afterwards Calvert wished to see me about something and came down under the stage just before the interval. He was alarmed to find no one in the pit, most of the orchestra were playing cards in the band-room. "Come, come, gentlemen," said the producer excitedly, "you will be late for the curtain music." The dealer paused and said, "We have nothing to play till the second part." "Nonsense," shouted Calvert,

"I have heard it every night—the hurry!" The musicians considered, and one admitted: "We did play something at the dress-rehearsal but only that once," and went on calmly with the game. Poor Calvert had been a victim of his own fine imagination; I am sure he never forgave us.

After the not-unsuccessful run at the Aldwych, Hackett took the whole show to Paris, making a few changes in the cast, as he said, in self-defence. We were to give one performance only, at the Odéon, where you must either have a big-band or none; and so I had all the string parts quadruplicated and they pulled up the floorboards and filled the pit with players—some of them my old friends from the Mogador. For some reason unknown to us, J.K. was to be installed as a Chevalier de la Légion d'Honneur after the performance. It was a very "matey" show; there were no palm leaves over the pit and no orchestra rail; the French President was there and all fashionable Paris filled the stalls, keeping up lively conversations with the orchestra in the intervals. After Part One we played, somewhat to their surprise, a "selection" of Norman's music; when we had finished, there was much applause but no sign of life from the stage. An obese senator nudged me heavily in the ribs—"Go round and see how long they are going to be," he growled. I went on to the stage. Hackett was in his shirt sleeves chatting amiably to a crowd of ladies, but there were no signs of setting our great Cauldron Scene, for which there was here plenty of room. I went back and reported to my fat nudger, who announced confidently that they would be half an hour.

So I took the orchestra over to the Foyot for a drink which they voted handsome, and we were back in plenty of time for the second part. The audience spotted my male witches among the musicians and joined cheerfully in with their Ho! Ho! Ho!'s, causing merriment in somewhat inappropriate places, but the evening finished triumphantly, and Hackett went off to the Chatham bearing proudly on his breast the glittering insignia of the Légion d'Honneur.

I give, without guarantee, an apocryphal duologue between the two Guitrys, said to have been overheard in the bar of "Teddy the VIIth":—

Sacha. "Strange all this fuss. I have played many times in London—but here comes this Yankee, gives one performance and goes away with the Croix."

Uncle Lucien. "My boy, let us not be ungrateful. He *did* go away, and he *did* only play it once."

Sacha. "Prosit."

Norman later on had another house near the village of Ewhurst in Surrey. It consisted of two Elizabethan farm cottages converted into one manor-house with a pond full of lilies outside the front door, and lower down a lawn upon which his little daughter Yvonne used to love to cheat me at croquet. Norman and I would take the train on Sunday morning to Horsley and walk across the Downs, talking music the while or solving those early crosswords appearing in the *Observer* under the pseudonym of Torquemada, who was a brother Savage called Powys Mather. They were pretty difficult and it was considered smart to get one finished by lunch time.

The country house was intended by Adine to be a rural extension of the studio in the Kensington garden, but I never saw Norman do any work there. He sweated at the rockery and dug like Adam himself in his flowerbeds and vegetable garden, but I don't think he actually put down much music, however richly he might have been storing his brain. In the evening we sat round the ingle in which there was a wood fire that was never allowed really to go out and talked again about men and music. Adine would sometimes play for us—perhaps a little Scarlatti—Alessandro as well as Domenico.

An idyllic life, which Fate suddenly shattered with one blow. Norman was walking along Oxford Street—nose in air—his head full of the tunes he was writing for *Twelfth Night.* He stepped off the pavement to cross Holles Street when a boy with a carrier tricycle ran into him and knocked him down. They laid him unconscious on the pavement, took the boy's name and address and sent for the ambulance. The first words Norman spoke when he recovered consciousness in the hospital were to exonerate the boy.

"It wasn't his fault," he gasped, "I should have looked where I was going."

I held up his job for him at the Alhambra and we all hoped and hoped each day for his recovery but it was not to be. Dear Norman, I often think of his handsome enthusiastic face and snow-white hair, and it is hard to believe that if he were with us now he would be eighty.

You will hear, later in this book, of my work with him in the "Phil", or to give it its proper and respectful title "The Royal Philharmonic Society".

CHAPTER XVI

Ellaline Terriss and Seymour Hicks

★

AT THE END of Chapter Ten I told of Charles Hamilton's introducing me to Seymour Hicks, and during the First World War it brought him back into my life, beginning with an engagement with his charming wife, Ellaline Terriss.

Ella was touring a little sketch, with music, I think, by Frank Tours, and Hamilton sent me to her as general manager and conductor. It was a very easy comfortable job, the boss was charming, considerate, and a great favourite with the public wherever she went; I had plenty of spare time and amused myself in thinking out advertising dodges that would boost the show.

The halycon days passed and I was to be exposed to the storm, that is to say, transferred to Seymour Hicks to manage and conduct *Scrooge*. Hicks had had made for him a forty minute sketch of Dickens's formidable old man with incidental music by Dora Bright, with which he toured the provincial music halls as top-of-the-bill from 1901 onwards. He submerged himself so deeply in the part that it was impossible to get a civil word out of him after he had once begun to make his nose up.

At his first entrance to his office on Christmas Eve, there was a piece of music which terminated in a loud sharp chord as he suddenly turned and stared at his clerk Cratchit. He had a habit of casting a prior glance over his shoulder before turning, with the foul intent of trapping the conductor into coming in too soon with the chord; this caught me, but only once. Later on I had to rehearse another man to conduct, an Irishman, and I warned him of the trap, marking the score, "Wait till Mr. Hicks turns *right* round."

The merciless Seymour tried the trap but the Irishman just grinned. Seymour grinned in reply and turned to face the conductor with a stamp, but still no chord and the music died out. After the performance, there was a fiery inquisition, but Pat was undisturbed. "Mr. Irving wrote," he said, " 'Wait till Mr. 'Icks turns roight round,' and you only turned half-way round." "What did you expect," said Hicks, "a pirouette?" "I work to orders," said the Irishman, "and if you mean half-way round, you should say half-way round." "Fair enough," said the boss, and they were firm friends ever afterwards.

Scrooge finished after a series of visions with Hicks rolling about the stage in an agony of penitence shouting "Lights, lights," which was quite a natural cue for the lime-light man to turn up his arc. At Bristol one night nothing happened and I could see the lime-light man on his perch leaning forward with his mouth open, engrossed with the acting. "Lights, lights," shouted Hicks fortissimo, and the fascinated operator's ringency still expanded. Eventually, the stage manager had to run up the iron ladder and turn on the arc. There was a tremendous curtain, and afterwards the wretched man was put on the carpet. "I'm sorry, Guv," he said, "but I was that fascinated that I forgot all about me lamp." "All right," said Seymour, "I'll forgive you this once," and in the next town he said to his stage director, "You know, Harry, that isn't a bad dodge with the lime-light man. Will you rehearse it with this one and have him well in view of the audience?"

Once you knew Seymour, he was a grand fellow to work for, and I wrote the music for many of his plays including *Old Bill, M.P.*, Bruce Bairnsfather's second play which was done at the Lyceum in 1922. I learned a tremendous amount from him about the tricks and uses of theatrical incidental music. He was difficult to please, but, unlike Basil Dean, always knew when he had got what he wanted.

During the First World War, he wrote a musical play called *Cash on Delivery*, with music by Haydn Wood, which I conducted at the Palace Theatre in 1917, displacing Herman Finck for the nonce. One night there was a Zeppelin raid and at the end of the show no "all clear" had been sounded; the audience were requested to retain their seats while we entertained them with music and the "bioscope", as moving pictures were then called. No "all clear" ever did come. The audience drifted away, and Seymour, Ella and I strolled down Shaftesbury Avenue with the idea of getting a sandwich at Appenrodt's in Piccadilly Circus.

When we were in the middle of the Circus the missing Zeppelin landed a bomb on Swan & Edgar's, blew out all the fine hats and dresses and scattered a shower of glass all over the pavements. It came tinkling down for five minutes after the bang.

All the waiters at Appenrodt's ran for their lives and we had the restaurant to ourselves. Seymour climbed over the bar, cut the sandwiches and opened a bottle of Burgundy. No one appeared to take the money and he counted it out carefully and registered it in the cash desk. When we emerged, glass was still tinkling down and we had to walk a quarter of a mile before a taxi would come near enough—a queer end to a very eerie evening.

There are, literally, thousands of stories about Sir Seymour; he has told most of them himself. But here is one which I'll bet he hasn't. We were playing in Manchester, staying at the Midland, and one night Seymour arrived after the show, very late, for supper with two friends. He had arranged the menu in the afternoon but something went wrong and Seymour called the waiter a d—— fool. "Really, Seymour," said Lady Hicks. "But think of the trouble I took," complained her husband, "and look at what we've got! He is a d—— fool." Ellaline rose to leave and I heard her swear for the first time. "Of course he is a d—— fool, Seymour, or he would not be waiting on you at one o'clock in the morning."

Seymour wanted very much to try his hand on serious parts, particularly Shakespeare, but the nearest he got was *David Garrick* in 1913, in which occurred the battle scene from *Richard III*. In this, Seymour, playing King Richard, had a sword fight with Bolingbroke, and he engaged Berteaux the fencer as his opponent, so that he could slash about as freely as he wished. One night, at the Coliseum, Berteaux turned up a little merry, and missing a double-handed skelp from the boss was irrevocably knocked out. The battle of Bosworth Field had to be finished somehow: King Richard, taking a leaf from Trebonius' book, seized his opponent's sword and stabbed himself to the sacrum.

Seymour was associated, of course, with nearly all George Edwardes' musical successes at the Gaiety, and afterwards made a great many for himself, such as *The Catch of the Season* (1904), *The Beauty of Bath* (1906), and *The Gay Gordons* (1907), the last of which I was destined to take on tour myself. I wrote the music for most of his other plays and sketches, and our greatest adventure together was the concert given at the India Office to the French President just before the outbreak of the Second World War.

Our diplomats had been entertained at a huge banquet in Paris, and it was planned to offer hospitality to the French in return, to be concluded by a grand entertainment, for which the courtyard of the India Office was covered in and fitted up as a theatre. Everything was planned upon a gigantic scale. Sir Seymour was put in charge, and he sent for me and handed over all the musical arrangements. "The first thing I must do," said I, "is to get a first-class orchestra."

"The first thing you must do," said Seymour, "is to get a first-class dress suit. Don't go to one of the fashionable society tailors, go to Morris Angel, he will make you something that will fit the occasion."

Morris, with his brother Louis, made nearly all the uniforms and smart male clothing seen in the West-end theatres and knew exactly what was wanted; he soon had me encased in a shiny dapper wasp-like garment, just a little too tight everywhere for a conductor's comfort. The job finished, he regarded me with affectionate admiration. "What about decorations?" he queried.

"I am sorry, Morris, I haven't any."

"Lou," he shouted downstairs to his brother, "what about that Victoria Cross that came in the other day?"

"Are you suggesting that I wear it at the concert?"

"Why not? Everybody will have medals of some sort."

"And what exactly would I be saying if His Majesty asked me where I won it?"

"Tell him Rorke's Drift," said the unblushing tailor, and I really believe he was half serious.

A good deal more than a dress suit was required for the concert. Seymour put up a tremendous display and I soon found myself landed with a symphony orchestra, the B.B.C. Singers and Choir, a whole forest of harpists and the full band of the Grenadier Guards, conductor and all.

This last attraction brought a little trouble in its train, as Major George Muller, Bandmaster of the Grenadiers, took a dim view of being directed by a civilian. But as he was a brother Savage, the delicate balance of precedence was soon settled over luncheon. "My dear fellow," said the Major, "however eminent you may be in the theatre world, I am Senior Bandmaster of the British Army and it is not decent for me to appear before their Majesties in a subordinate position." "Nothing could be more simple," I said. "You do the conducting and I will follow your beat." And so it was. When their Majesties entered with their guests, George Muller appeared with his men in the grand gallery and started the long regulation drum-roll;

I followed him from below, successfully synchronising my mixed and massed forces to his sweeping beat.

Lord Halifax, Lord Vansittart and Lord Hood, who were at the head of affairs, did not much like the idea of having the Guards and thought that Seymour was overdoing it in the way of sound effects. "Besides," said Lord Hood, "the Guards will drop cigarette-ends all over the place. Can't you manage without them?" But I was not going to let Seymour down and reminded Lord Hood that we were only using the band of the Grenadiers, and that there were quite a number of Guardsmen free to follow the band round and pick up their cigarette-ends, and I must say that, from the point of view of display, the entrance of the Guards provided a grand moment.

The India Office on the night of the concert was a marvellous spectacle, blazing with jewels and gorgeous with robes and coronets brought out for the occasion. I dare say some of it was paste, but I have never seen such a glittering, scintillating display, and I doubt if many like it will ever be seen again. Mr. Churchill, who was present as First Lord of the Admiralty, wore, I think, a magnificent uniform, all over broad gold lace, and the tremendous pomp of the audience completely dwarfed the pleasant little entertainment which I thought somewhat on the dull side. However, all went well and the gigantic ensemble moved through its appointed manoeuvres without hitch or flaw. When the entertainment was over, I sat on my rostrum talking to Laurence Irving, who was in Court dress and smoking a cigarette. He dropped the fag-end upon the floor. A sad-faced corporal of the Guards, carrying a silver salver, approached at slow march tempo, picked it up and departed.

Sir Seymour came out to Ealing later on to make a film, a very good film, too, but he was really too good an actor to make a successful film star. We had, however, by no means finished our work together, because when His Majesty's Government organised E.N.S.A. to keep the troops cheerful, he and Basil Dean were placed in charge of it and duly impressed me as musical director, of which more anon.

From Sir Seymour I learned, I think, all there is to know about the employment of incidental music in comedy and melodrama, and this proved to be of great use in the film studio. I also got the strongest confirmation of Edward German's postulate that once the curtain has touched the stage there must be no chord except tonic and dominant.

CHAPTER XVII

My Brass Plate

★

A CARPENTER FRIEND of mine, from Ealing Studios, is, at this moment, screwing on to my bedroom door a brass place which has accompanied me round the London theatres during the last forty years. I got this idea from Herman Finck, who always had one on his door in whatever theatre he was operating, and I thought it gave a pleasant, if illusive, idea of security of tenure and long runs, so I had engraved on a plate with big black capitals on the golden brass, about 12″ x 3″, "ERNEST IRVING MUSICAL DIRECTOR", and the first time I got a chance had it affixed to my door with six brass screws.

The following list of theatres at which I have worked shows some of its resting places. It did not accompany me to all of them, and when I came to the Ealing Studios in 1933 I had it put up there:—

ADELPHI	*The Way of an Eagle* (1922)
	The Laughing Cavalier (1937)
	International Ballet (1947)
ALDWYCH	*Hamlet in modern dress* (1925)
	The Marvellous History of St. Bernard (1926)
	Macbeth (J. K. Hackett) (1920)
ALHAMBRA	Shakespearean Season (1934)
AMBASSADORS	*The Two Bouquets* (1936)
	The Curate's Egg ('orrid memory) (1922)

CAMBRIDGE	*Hansel and Gretel* (with real rabbits) (1933)
CASINO	International Ballet (1948)
COLISEUM	International Ballet (1946)
DOMINION	Revival of *The Land of Smiles* (1932)
DUKE OF YORKS	*Toto*
DRURY LANE	Tauber in *The Land of Smiles* (1931)
EMPIRE	*The Lilac Domino* (1918)
	The Red Mill (with Little Tich)
	Variety Season, etc., etc.
GAIETY	*Riki-Tiki*
GARRICK	*Dedé* (1922)
HAYMARKET	*Yellow Sands* (1926)
HER MAJESTY'S	*The Dubarry* (1932)
	Beau Geste (1928)
	Henry IV (with George Robey) (1935)
	International Ballet (1945)
HIPPODROME	*The Maid of the Mountains* (1930)
KINGSWAY	*Polly* (1923)
	Hamlet in Modern Dress (1925)
	An Elephant in Arcady (1938)
LONDON PAVILION	*This Year of Grace* (1928)
	Wake up and Dream (1929)
LYCEUM	*Old Bill, M.P.* (1922)
LYRIC	*Lilac Time* (1922)
	Autumn Crocus (1931)
NEW	*The Circle of Chalk* (1929)
	Johnson Over Jordan (1939)
NEW OXFORD	*Kismet* (1925)
PALACE	*Cash on Delivery* (1917)
PICCADILLY	*The Student Prince* (1929)
PRINCES	*The Catch of the Season* (1917)
	International Ballet (1945)
QUEEN'S	*The Immortal Hour* (1932)
REGENT	*The Insect Play* (1923)

ST. JAMES'S	*The Glass Slipper* (1944)
SAVILLE	*Johnson over Jordan* (1939)
SAVOY	*An Elephant in Arcady* (1938)
SHAFTESBURY	*Castles in the Air*
	The Chocolate Soldier (1932)
WESTMINSTER	*The Cure for Love* (1945)

For the open air theatre in Regent's Park, where we did Mozart's *Figaro and Così Fan Tutte* in 1938, there was no door on which I could have fixed my brass plate, as my headquarters were in a tent, and you could not have screwed it to a tree.

Talking about brass plates, there is a little story about W. H. Berry who, having been injected into a dying play at the Adelphi too late to save it, was fixing his plate on to his dressing-room door, and sent his dresser to borrow a hammer from the stage-door keeper. The messenger was a long while gone, but when questioned about the delay, said that the stage-door keeper was using it and he had to wait. "Using it," said Berry, "what for?" "To nail up the fortnight's notice," said the dresser.

During my brass plate's long stay at the Lyric for *Lilac Time* in the amiable company of Clara Butterworth, Charie (Courtice) Pounds, and Edmund Gwenn, many amusing things happened. At the dress rehearsal, some members of the public were invited, and the orchestra were requested to wear evening dress. The first horn player did not get the instruction, and turned up in a blue shirt. He was requested by the management to rectify this, and took from a nail in the band-room an indiarubber shirt-front, with celluloid white tie attached, which had been left there by a player of the outgoing orchestra. On the last night of the long run, I asked the orchestra to drink with me in the band-room, and before he picked up his glass, he carefully sponged the faithful "dickey", and replaced it on the peg, saying: "You never know, it might be useful to the next man." For all I know it is there still.

One night, King George V and Queen Mary visited the show with the King and Queen of Norway, and I received instructions from an equerry that the King did not wish the National Anthem to be played either before, during, or after the performance; consequently, when the curtain fell, I proceeded to play the "Flower Waltz" which George Clutsam had "arranged" from Schubert. There was an old Brigadier in the stalls who drew himself up to attention for the National Anthem; he glared fiercely at me, came over and made a heated protest, saying I should be ashamed of myself. I referred him to the Centurion in the Bible and showed him my orders. "Dear, dear," said the old boy, "how extraordinary. I would not have thought it of them," and departed spluttering, and complaining to the manager on his way out, though I do not suppose King George got the message!

This episode brings to mind some other memories of royalty. Queen Victoria I only saw once, at Osborne during a very youthful visit to Cowes regatta, a sad old lady, small, stately and still; and I never got nearer to King Edward VII than when his funeral procession passed the theatre where I was rehearsing *Merrie England* for a company of London amateurs. We stopped our noise, of course, for the procession to pass; it was strange to hear the guardsmen's dirge after "Long Live Elizabeth".

King Alfonso of Spain I have written about in another chapter; he was very kind to us in Madrid and we saw a lot of him. He was friendly and courteous, entirely without side, a good sportsman in spite of the bullfights, and a grand loser at bridge. The Queen was different; she was just as kind and gracious as her husband, but had more of the "royal" touch and stood a little aloof.

King George V often came to special shows and Queen Mary until her last illness was a constant theatre-goer. She was a tower of strength to the music director of "Royal" matinées, the *tiniest* nod behind her programme giving the hint that *one* encore would be sufficient so that he could get on and finish the matinée before dinner-time.

King George V knew what he liked and what he did not like. He had a big gruff bass voice and expressed his opinions, especially if adverse, freely and with great sonority. I remember one matinée at His Majesty's Theatre where Sir Gerald du Maurier was appearing. I had, as usual, planted an extra trombone player on a high seat under the royal box with instructions to take plenty of bars' rest and listen for any *jeux d'esprit* from the royal lips. We had played the National Anthem, after which Sir Thomas Beecham took my place, performed the overture to *Figaro* in world's record time—one minute 50 and one-fifth seconds, I think—and disappeared. The King had just time to discard some garments and settle down in his seat. "That was Sir Thomas Beecham conducting Mozart," said Queen Mary. "Oh, was it?" said the King looking up to give Sir Thomas a nod, but there was nothing there except perhaps a faint whiff of brimstone!

The King scanned his programme—"Ha," said he, "here is du Maurier palming off that old sketch in which the revolver doesn't go off—I've seen it about five times. They think they can fob me off with anything." "Hush, dear," said the Queen. "Let us see."

Now this was a *new* sketch in which the revolver did go off, but believe it or not, it missed fire six times. The sketch limped to a tame finish. "What did I tell you?" roared King George, and stamped off into the tea-room. He was no cynic, though, and I often saw him, when he was satisfied, express his approval with equal vigour; but in the realm of music he liked tunes simple and melodious.

CHAPTER XVIII

Frederic Austin and Nigel Playfair

★

EXCEPTING POSSIBLY Thomas Beecham, Frederic Austin was the most surprising man I ever got to know. One knew he was a baritone of pleasant sound and an actor of parts, but it was not until a look had been taken at the inside of his scores that one realised that here was a genius; not on the grand scale, perhaps, but one whose work, in its small way, was as exquisite as that of Mozart. Composers who reset *The Beggar's Opera* will find this out for themselves.

When Nigel Playfair took the Euston Music Hall and turned it into the Regent Theatre, he opened it in 1923 with *The Insect Play* of Karel Capek; Austin wrote the incidental music and I conducted. I liked his music, he liked my interpretation of it, and when Eugene Goossens, after conducting *Polly* for a few weeks, retired to bigger things, I was asked to take his place. There followed an enduring friendship which lasted through several years of association in the theatres and upon the Royal Philharmonic Society and Delius Trust committee until Austin's death.

Polly was a delightful score to conduct, and, but for the untimely death of Pitt Chatham, might have run a year. Austin wanted very much to conduct it for a week or two himself and asked me to direct *The Beggar's Opera* for a fortnight at the Lyric Theatre, Hammersmith, so that he could "have a go" at *Polly* which was running merrily at the Kingsway.

I knew *The Beggar's Opera* backwards, having seen it many

times the proper way, namely, one act at a time and the other two in the bar, and when I was offered a rehearsal, I declined with thanks. "I do not want to rehearse a company that has been playing for over one thousand nights, and still less do I want them to rehearse me," I wrote, and this led to a misunderstanding which makes a little story.

On the summer night appointed, I donned my dress clothes, put on a big cigar and strolled hatless to the Lyric stage door. The doorkeeper barred my entrance, misled probably by the Bolivar, and asked me to wait outside, which I did, sitting on a wooden form surveying the traffic in the market. Presently there was a hullabaloo inside, and my friend Stephen Thomas, the stage director, rushed by. "Hello, Ernest," said he, "you have seen *The Beggar's Opera* dozens of times, do you think you could conduct it because Mr. Morris has gone away on holiday and has forgotten to send a deputy?" "Well," I replied, "to conduct *The Beggar's Opera* was my immediate object in life but our friend here, doing no more than his duty, won't let me in." As I always conducted everything from memory, I had the conductor's stand removed, which I am sure the ladies who formed the excellent little orchestra thought a piece of swank, as indeed I suppose it was.

Apparently nobody had been warned of my invasion, and the Beggar sent down to find out my name, so that he could give me the cue: "Now, Mr. Irving, play up the overture!"

When I entered the orchestra there was a little buzz of expectation from the faithful audience, most of whom were acquainted with every detail of the opera. Pepusch's overture opened with a harpsichord solo, and there sat Miss Nellie Chaplin, the famous player, severe profile, chignon north to south, waiting for my down beat. The Beggar spoke the Prologue, the beat came down—and not a sound from the harpsichord.

I glared in surprise at the unimpressed Nellie and turned to her sister Kate, who was leading, for an explanation. While I had my back to her, the harpsichord started by itself, and I found out afterwards that the conductor should wait till the Beggar had made his exit before beginning the music. But this kindness was too ignominious to be borne, and when the ladies offered me in the interval tea from their thermi (if that is the plural of thermos) I declined, and said I was very surprised to find them making me so uncomfortable. This scandalously false accusation actually brought tears, but I explained that like Sir Thomas Beecham I never "appeared to conduct", and if they wanted me to be happy they would have to let me make any mistake I fancied in my own way. After all these performances this must have been very difficult for them, but I am bound to say they carried it out, and judging by the audience the little freshness that it brought to the show was appreciated. I thoroughly enjoyed my stay and was almost sorry when the time came to go back to *Polly*.

Austin was as meticulous in his scoring as Edward German. I gave him some film music to write for *Midshipman Easy* at Ealing Studios and found him very inflexible to work with; he seemed to think that the film should be shot to fit the music. I see that in a recent book Dr. Vaughan Williams puts forward something of the same kind, but, of course, only a very small proportion of the people from whom the cinema revenues come is musical, and films must not be treated as if they were operas. I often think the most difficult job in the film industry is that of the man who has to sell the films.

It was through Austin that I came to conduct *Lilac Time*, which ran for two years at the Lyric, Shaftesbury Avenue. Such a long engagement is a soul-destroying affair, even with a little Schubert thrown in, but if the conductor is to have security of tenure, he cannot expect excitement as well.

Playfair's adventures away from Hammersmith did not prosper and the Regent Theatre passed into the hands of Sir Barry Jackson of Birmingham, of whom more later.

CHAPTER XIX

On Getting the Sack for the Fourth and Last Time

★

THIS IS A little chapter about a little man who took a little theatre to produce a little play which only ran a little while. It produced a very little sack, but it was a definite unmistakable sack—backed up by a formal fortnight's notice—and it was not caused so much by any incompetence on my part as by the workings of jazz in the bowels of my employer.

The time was the early 'twenties, and the executioner was Nelson Keys, a tiny comedian whose strong point was the impersonation of other actors; he had upon his record many successes in Sir Alfred Butt's revues. The witty librettist Arthur Wimperis, who had half-maliciously nicknamed him Bunch, had written a play for him in which he could launch out for himself. Herman Finck composed the music, which he scored for a little orchestra of ten, a tight fit for the pit at the Ambassadors'.

They called it *The Curate's Egg*, which was taking a risk, especially as the play lived up to its name and was good only in parts. Finck's score was in his best "Gilbert the Filbert" style, but since the Palace days, musical comedy had been subverted by jazz, and to tell the truth Herman was a little out of date. So for that matter was I.

Keys was a red-hot jazz fan. At home in his drawing-room he had a complete set of jazz percussion with which he ruined the repose of any infant or invalid within half a mile; my drummer at the Ambassadors' was to him like a Roman relic. Nevertheless, Keys stalked boldly through the play, and its fate trembled in the balance.

Keys was very popular in fashionable society and managed to get for *The Curate's Egg* a boost which certainly should have saved it. It came in the form of an invitation from Lady Ancaster to perform the whole play, lock, stock and barrel, at her house in Kensington. She was giving a big party and her guests included the four Royal Princes—the Prince of Wales and the Dukes of York, Gloucester and Kent. All went well, but after the performance was over the Prince of Wales asked me if "my boys would play for a little dancing." I said that we should be delighted to try, but that my little band was composed of symphony orchestra players who knew very little about jazz.

Of course, we were most anxious to put up a show; so I sent a messenger scurrying round for some music, and meanwhile we played from memory, not very well, I'm afraid, any of the popular foxtrots we could recollect. It was a long time before anybody thought of asking Keys to join in the fun; he would probably have been more effectual with his jazz kit alone. The dancing gradually faded down and the dancers drifted to the bar, where the Princes called the musicians to refreshment and thanked them for their efforts. They were most polite and I think in a sort of children's-party-way enjoyed the fun, but Keys was furious and I detected a certain gelidity in Lady Ancaster's valediction.

In the theatre, Keys became more and more hostile. He began tapping out the rhythm with his walking stick and I retaliated very naughtily by tapping it on my desk. He wanted me to sack my timpanist and engage a jazz professor and to replace the clarinet by a saxophone. He tried to get Finck to conduct himself, but Herman was not taking any such risk, and when I was served with two weeks' notice to "terminate my engagement" he engaged Sydney Baynes, composer of two famous waltzes, to take my place.

Sydney was a great friend of mine; I stood him a lunch and gave him due warning. He was very superior and told me that I did not know how to handle Bunch. "Patience is what you require," said the wiseacre, "and you are foolish to have signed a contract with a fortnight's notice in it. I have got an agreement for the run of the play." Well, I do not say that it was cause and effect, but after I left the play ran one week, and I got two weeks' salary in lieu of notice. I was very angry with Bunch and contemplated taking action against him, but with this *dénouement* the quarrel dissolved in laughter and I actually made a little financial gain out of being sacked for the fourth and last time, so that there is no moral to be drawn from this chapter at all, I fear.

CHAPTER XX

Cochran and Coward

★

My first introduction to "Cocky" was almost as startling as that to Edwardes. "C.B." had a successful revue running at the London Pavilion with Spinelli and Anne Croft in the cast. It contained three short ballets, in which Massine and Karsavina danced. The conductor was suddenly taken ill and rushed off to hospital for an operation. C.B. had a very useful musical lieutenant, Elsie April, a talented woman, who deserved a great deal more credit than she ever got for the work she did, including the bold deed I am about to relate.

I was conducting a short revue at the Palladium for Sidney Low which was finishing that weekend, and Elsie telephoned me, inviting me to take over the Spinelli show at the latest on the following Monday. Always prepared for an adventure, I gleefully accepted, and saw what I could of the Spinelli show in the spare time between my own three weekend performances.

Now it is quite impossible to accompany a revue, let alone a ballet, and learn a score at the same time, so on Saturday evening, having settled my accounts at the Palladium, I collected the score and took it home to Highgate to memorise, a process I carried out mostly on a seat in Waterlow Park, to the great amusement of the children playing there. I have always been blessed with a phenomenal memory; and have improved it to a point of virtuosity by blindfold chess-playing; but as this revue contained about forty musical numbers, including three ballets, I found it a tough proposition and following my usual practice decided not to have the score on the desk at all, in case I should be tempted to open it. I refused the offer of a Monday rehearsal, as I knew it would make me nervous, and concentrated so much that I left my despatch case containing Sidney Low's balance of profit for the week on the Highgate tramcar. I never got it back, and had to make it up out of my own pocket, with gratitude to the Gods that I did not leave the score there as well.

The performance, you may be sure, was very interesting for everyone concerned; Cocky and Elsie were scared of the vacant desk, and the artistes were also most surprised to find a conductor looking at them with his nose in the air, instead of in the score. The whole thing came off surprisingly well, as the Fates granted the stroke of luck which was necessary, and I made very good friends at that performance.

There was one ballet which gave me a shock. It was called "The Tale of a Tub" and it was an arrangement of a Haydn Symphony by my friend Norman O'Neill. Massine made an entrance marked "O.P." in the score, with a drum roll, and landed on a cymbal note to start his dance. I started the drum roll and looked anxiously for Massine, when he suddenly arrived, flying through the air, twelve feet up, I was so startled that I came down, whack, with the cymbal at exactly the right moment to a split second, which I was told afterwards had never been done before.

I thus started a reputation for ballet conducting which was to serve me in good stead later on, and which was greatly enhanced by my getting Karsavina's famous thirty-six *fouettées* exactly to her liking; also, I believe, a novelty. My friend the conductor, I am happy to say, recovered after a few weeks, and I handed him back his job, but my *tour de force* had got me in with Cochran, and he gave me shortly afterwards a nauseous job, to conduct an American musical. *Castles in the Air* was, I believe, produced in Chicago—a most appropriate place of origin. Its intellectual content was nil, and I was very surprised that Cochran had anything to do with it at all, but he had a rare vision of the future in all he did, and probably foresaw the swamping of London with the American musicals which we enjoy—or suffer—at the present time.

Castles in the Air opened at the Blackpool Opera House. The opening went off with great *éclat*. During the first performance I played a blindfold game of chess with the principal 'cellist, who used a little pocket board. I was able, towards the end of the second act, to announce a brilliant mate in six moves, which the 'cellist—a good sportsman—took to the local paper, who published it. The Press notices of *Castles in the Air* were first-rate; Cocky himself was delighted with the performance, and said so; but one of the London papers got hold of the chess-game played during the performance, and compared it with a game of the great Paul Morphy, and it was printed and re-printed in nearly all the chess columns all over the world.

Cocky received one of these press cuttings, which gave him a sort of crescendo of annoyance, until I think he began to believe that I had neglected conducting entirely in order to enjoy my game. When the piece some time afterwards did come to London, where it failed dismally, he made me give him my word of honour not even to think chess during the performance. Of course, he did not understand, what I shall explain in another chapter, that chess-playing does not in the least interfere with musical control, and, in fact, gives a sort of fulcrum against which concentration may make its driving thrust.

Cochran was planning a new kind of revue (for 1928) with a much stronger intellectual voltage, the book and most of the music to be written by Noel Coward, who was then a little under a cloud, having had one or two failures after his first great success. Cochran thought that I was the man to handle Noel and his music. He was very nearly right, but not quite.

Now Coward as a writer of light humorous lyrics is in the

first class; as a composer of light music, in the third class; as a musician in the sixth class; and as a singer—nowhere. Nevertheless, he frequently sings his own songs, and they survive it, so there must be something in them, besides the lyric.

We had to play over *This Year of Grace* in Cochran's drawing-room, and Willie Boosey, head of Chappell's, was present. Obese, good-humoured, and lethargic after luncheon, Boosey went to sleep during the first act; when it was all finished, the audience woke him up and asked his opinion, and he, not unnaturally, referred them to me.

I said that the lyrics were the best I had ever heard since Basil Hood, and that he ought to print them. Boosey said: "Nonsense! No-one would buy them nowadays." I bet him a fiver that he would sell a thousand in the first week, and mentioned that in any case they would be useful for rehearsals. There were three or four numbers which were obviously good, in spite of Coward's barbarous vocalisation "A Room with a View", "Dance Little Lady", etc. Needless to say I won my fiver hands down, as the lyrics were brilliant, in Coward's best style.

Tilly Losch was in the show, and had a dance in front of a church window, set to the Bach "Aria for the G string", and we used to tease Noel at rehearsals by saying "Ah! that is the best tune in the show!"—which indeed it was! A slight flavour of the all-conquering jazz was imported by having "Hutch" in the orchestra playing the piano, and one clarinet who doubled a little on the saxophone. But I firmly resisted any attempts to "modernise" the music, though there was a little syncopation in "Dance Little Lady".

This Year of Grace, with Jessie Matthews, Sonnie Hale, and Maisie Gay, had a preliminary run in Manchester, and was, of course, an enormous success. The tired tradesmen who filled the stalls did not take kindly to Bach, and the aria to which Tilly danced was nearly cut out for London. However, a last-minute petition to Cocky kept it in, which was indeed a very lucky thing, not only for her, but for Noel and all of us, as it was the highspot of the first night success at the London Pavilion.

All my first nights with Cochran were exciting, and this one was no exception. There had been a few last-minute alterations, and the copyist—an old half-blind Scots master—was left in the band room to make the necessary alteration in the band parts. I followed my usual procedure—a sleep in the afternoon, a bath, a porterhouse steak, a *soufflée* and a bottle of Chambertin at the "Cavour"—and strolled into the band room through a stormy evening for a chat to the orchestra. My librarian was waiting for me with a white face. "Home has disappeared with half the music," he gasped.

It seemed that the cleaners had annoyed Home at his work, and he had retired to a more comfortable spot—but where? He lived in Camberwell, but I hazarded a guess that he might have gone to a copying bureau that sometimes employed him, in Shaftesbury Avenue. A telephone message proved me to be right and that he had just left for the London Pavilion. My librarian hastened to meet him, and they collided outside the Apollo, where Home was enlisting the help of passing pedestrians to retrieve some sheets of music which had blown into the gutter while he clasped the rest to his breast in the wind and rain.

Now Cochran had notified the Press and all concerned that the show would commence promptly at 8 p.m. and asked them all to be seated by five minutes to eight as the opening was important, and, believe it or not, every seat in the Pavilion was occupied at three minutes to eight when Cochran came down the aisle, patted me on the back as I stood at the conductor's desk, and pulled out his gold repeater. I smiled broadly at him, and said quietly, "Charles, please do not turn a hair—we cannot start as there is no music in the theatre, but it is on its way and I want you, please, to look as delighted as I do." Cocky did his best to rival Mona Lisa; I pulled my watch and wagged my head in a hilarious negative. The librarian arrived and whispered hoarsely, "Its all here, Guv'nor," so I whispered, "Put it out quietly, and when everybody's settled, pinch my leg; meanwhile get the oboeist to sound a final A." I waited for, and received, the welcome pinch, we both pulled out our watches, nodded affirmatively, shook hands, and the overture started for the most successful revue Cocky ever staged—at 8.5 p.m.!

Since that little episode, I have never allowed any music, under any pretext, to be removed from the theatre during the run of the play.

In *This Year of Grace* there was a comic ballet, and as Maisie Gay was the prima ballerina, you may be sure it was comic. Elsie April had written several variations on Coward's theme and I used to improvise something new nearly every night in the style of one composer or another, depending largely upon whether there was any notability in front to whom it could be applied. The dancers loved the changes because it kept the thing spontaneous and alive, but when Coward returned from his holiday he expressed disapproval and we called a band rehearsal "to put it right". In self-defence I pointed out that the ballet was a great hit, but Coward insisted that it should be cut and dried. "All right then," I said, "which version would you like?—we have nine or ten." "I should like it as I wrote it," said Noel. So I sent Borsdorf the librarian to my room to get the original manuscript. Innocently (perhaps) he did bring the original manuscript without Elsie's variations, and I handed it to Noel with the remark: "Well there it is—it's very good but also I fear very short." On a half sheet of paper were sixteen bars in the treble clef.

I never got on very well with Noel after this and he did not ask me to conduct *Bitter Sweet*, which was splendidly arranged by Elsie and orchestrated by de Orellana, but I must do him justice by adding that he made Elsie a handsome present, which indeed she richly deserved.

Bitter Sweet being off as far as I was concerned, my next job in 1929 was at the London Pavilion—a revue called *Wake up and Dream* with music by Cole Porter. I flew to Paris to see the composer and found, as I feared, that the score was much too "jazzy" for my taste. I do not like that kind of music, and consequently I do not conduct it very well—in fact not at all if I can help it—but I had brought it upon myself. In the meantime Basil Dean gave me the job of writing the music for a production of *Beau Geste* at His Majesty's Theatre, and in a curious way, which I shall describe in the next chapter, this enabled me to escape the opening of *Wake up and Dream*.

In spite of all these ups and downs, Cocky and I remained firm friends. His tragic death came as a dreadful shock.

CHAPTER XXI

Anna May Wong

★

As I HAVE said, Basil Dean had asked me to write the music for *Beau Geste*, the famous drama by P. C. Wren, for His Majesty's Theatre. In view of my Cochran contract, I engaged another conductor for this, but at the dress rehearsal I received a message that he had been taken ill and that the band was sitting around doing nothing. I had been working very hard and very late and was feeling played out, but I dashed down to His Majesty's and took charge; we rehearsed all day and on through the night. I scarcely had time for a bath and change of raiment before the first performance. At the interval I was climbing up to the Bar with my librarian (another Borsdorf) to get a brandy and soda, but collapsed on the stairs with a heart attack. Mr. Borsdorf, very luckily for me, had a brother-in-law in front who was a doctor; he gave me an injection to get me through the rest of the show and ordered me then to go to bed and stay there.

The evening ended with a tragi-comedy. The play finished with what was called the "Viking's Funeral", when there was a tremendous fire on the stage with electric lights and coloured silk to make very realistic flames. The show ran late and an uninformed fireman coming on duty at eleven o'clock saw the flames, rushed on to the stage, rang down the fireproof curtain and set the sprinklers to work. Too late, he was suppressed by a furious stage-manager, who got the curtain up again for a very damp fizzle of a tag. The Press came round, and Dean explained why, and by whom, the curtain had been rung down. "I can understand that," said one of the critics, "what I want to know is, why and by whom it was rung up again!"

Strictly held in bed by the doctor, I was unable to conduct any more *Beau Geste* or to attend to the opening of *Wake up and Dream*. I was not heartbroken over that, though it is a bit boring to have to have a heart attack every time you do not like a job.

In 1929 Dean was planning the production of an old Chinese play translated by James Laver, *The Circle of Chalk*, in which Anna May Wong, the popular Chinese film actress, was to star. A lot of Chinese music was needed for the play, and this had been written, and very well written, by a young and popular composer, but the songs in *The Circle of Chalk* had to be sung by the actors, and the existing score, though very clever and tuneful, was much too difficult for them to sing—especially those for Anna May who had only four good notes in her voice. I was asked by Dean to adapt it. I found this impossible, but offered to write a new score to fit the voices available and use a really Chinese combination in the orchestra pit. This suited Dean, who believes in stunts of that kind, and I set to work, in bed, to compose it.

The first thing I did was to invent the orchestra, in which I proposed to have the following instruments:— one violin; one viola; one 'cello with two middle strings tuned up to two octaves higher; one double-bass with a metal mute; one harp (a virtuoso); one E-flat clarinet; one cor anglais; one bassoon; one trumpet in D; one harmonium—to be played by the conductor —and three wonderful percussion players, who must have a paragraph to themselves.

First of all there was a regular timpanist with bass drum, side drum, cymbals and all the usual drummer's battery—Beckwith of the London Symphony Orchestra. Then there was my young friend Julian Clifford; he is now a well-known conductor and I hope will not mind this reminiscence. He played five little tuned kettledrums, an ocarina, a mouth organ, all kinds and sizes of cymbals, a rolling marble in a cigar box, and various other Chinese gadgets. I also called on a very talented pianist of my acquaintance named Leslie Bridgewater. This young man performed with virtuosity on many instruments beside the piano, particularly on a big xylophone called a marimba, and he possessed the only bass oboe in London. He could play, in addition, the horn, saxophone and glockenspiel—so all these noises were incorporated in the score. I hoicked him down from Blyth where he was conducting at the local cinema and put the rehearsals in his charge.

Laurence Olivier was in the cast, playing a Prince with the intriguing name of "Po", and I wrote him a nice song, "A Wandering Blade", which I thought he sang very well, but the critics did not agree, and Dean cut half of it out to our sorrow. Frank Cochran (a good singer) had two nice songs; George Curzon and Bruce Winston one each. As for Anna May, she did splendidly with her numbers, in which I exploited her four tones in every kind of musical variation. If her acting had been as good as her singing, and her speaking of the English language a little less San Franciscan *The Circle of Chalk* might have run as long as *Chu Chin Chow*, but alas! it was not so. I dragged myself out of bed for the band rehearsals; up to then I had not heard a bar of my own music.

On the first night James Agate lifted the palm leaves under which the orchestra was hidden from the public view and said: "Oh, Ernest, I believe some of these tunes are genuine Chinese and some are your own—which are which?" I said: "Can't you tell, James?" "No," said he frankly, "I can't." "How lucky for me," I returned, and off he went.

The next man to lift the palm leaves was Frank Collins, C. B. Cochran's stage director, to wish me luck. But the next morning I received a note from the office to say that if I was well enough to conduct *The Circle of Chalk* I was well enough to conduct *Wake up and Dream*. So I left Bridgewater to take care of my Chinese score while I went back to the dreary round.

The Circle of Chalk stirred up considerable interest in Chinese music and I wrote for Anna May a little operatic sketch, incorporating her four good notes, called "The Red Watering Pot" which she played with success in every country in the world—including China!

I also composed a Chinese song-cycle, to verses translated by Edward Knoblock, entitled "Love Behind the Lattice" and set for two voices and orchestra. This was intended for my second wife, who has a beautiful contralto voice, but when the music was completed she did not like it much and it was broadcast by Gladys Ripley with Roderick Jones singing the baritone line and Charles Groves conducting. I listened in agony; not that it was not splendidly sung and played, but because I was held on the rack in my bedroom by a fierce attack of gout. Later on, we did a film at Ealing with Anna May in a Chinese milieu called *Java Head* but she did not have to sing in this.

My return to the London Pavilion was not for long as my heart again conked out. I was invalided to Ramsgate. When I recovered the *Dream* was over, and I went to Edward Laurillard to conduct a revival of *The Student Prince*.

CHAPTER XXII

My Railway Accident

★

The Student Prince was followed by *My Sister and I*, which was principally remarkable from my point of view for a first-class railway accident. Perhaps readers might find my recollection of this interesting; personally I was very disappointed with it and found it much less exciting than I had hoped, but there were some curious psychic features which may be worth relating.

I was travelling to Glasgow on the Royal Scot to conduct the first performance of *My Sister and I*. It was in March, 1931, and at Euston I did something that I had not done for years—I walked up the platform to have a look at the engine, where I found the engine-driver saying "Goodbye" to his wife and child. Perched on the tender behind him was an enormous block of coal as big as an armchair, and when he said "Good morning, sir," to me, I pointed to it and said "You must be careful not to run off the line or you will collect that lot." He asked: "Where are you sitting, sir?" "Oh!" I replied, "about five coaches down." Said he, "That's exactly where it would land!"

I thanked him, booked a ticket for the first luncheon, and when the train started commenced a game of chess with one of my musicians. Luncheon-time arrived, finding my opponent cornered and "exploring every avenue" of escape from a threatened mate. The train was going very fast and I amused myself, while waiting for him to move, in timing a mile, which took fifty-two seconds. All-of-a-sudden came a whistle and a jolt and I realised that we were bumping along off the rails. I said to my opponent quietly: "We are in for a smash. Put your feet up, as I believe the next coach has a habit of coming in and amputating them." He did so, there was a terrific screech "crescendo sostenuto", and the carriage turned over onto its side, tipping all the chessmen with glasses, plates and books into the lee-scuppers. I looked out of the window; ahead of us were four coaches thrown athwart the line and piled on top of each other. I said to my opponent: "We have just stopped in time to avoid running into some wreckage," but I found myself talking to no-one as he had joined the passengers who were clamouring at the door—now the roof—to be extricated. I looked again and realised that the piled-up wreckage was our own train, and as there was nothing better to do I began to pick up the chessmen, which I prized.

Rescue came and we emerged. Outside stood two Greek gentlemen and one of them addressed me excitedly, saying, "Am I 'urt, am I 'urt?" I said to him "You are not 'urt, but your 'air is full of glass—what 'appened to you?" Said the first Greek, "We were 'aving a drink in the refreshment car (this was the apex of the pile of wreckage) and I lift my glass and I say 'Prosit', the floor opens, we fall through many feet and we are standing on the engine!" A local lady invited us to a drink in her house, and we set off with the Greek brushing the glass out of his "'air", and nearly getting run over on the way. I telephoned my wife and said "I am not 'urt but the train has run off the line." "Yes," said she calmly, "I thought it would!"

I found it all singularly unexciting, but the sad part of it was that six people were killed, and the body of my friend the engine-driver was dragged out from under the mass of coal that we had joked about. Make what you like of this, but by my conversation with him I was able to establish at the inquiry that he was perfectly sober, and by the accidental wait for the chess move that the speed of the train was over seventy miles an hour. It appeared that the main line was up in Leighton Buzzard station and that the driver did not receive the proper information; the wretched signalman was in the dreadful dilemma of either letting the train crash on the points or come to equal disaster amongst the men working on the line, and he had no time to do anything.

We were put into some old coaches that were rotting on a siding and bumped off into Bletchley by an enormous express engine at such a speed that we all thought we were in for a second accident, which would have been too much for one day. However, we survived and got to Glasgow just in time for the band rehearsal.

I came out of it without a scratch but lost a black pawn; my saxophonist acquired a vibrato that I am informed lasted him a fortnight. Looking back upon the accident, it is strange how natural and matter of course it all seemed. Moral (from saxophonist): Never resign a game of chess as long as you have a move left.

CHAPTER XXIII

Barry Jackson and Bernard Shaw

★

SIR BARRY JACKSON'S invasion of London with *The Immortal Hour* was a really epoch-making affair. He had produced Rutland Boughton's faery opera in Birmingham with surprising success but most people thought his venture in the Metropolis a forlorn hope. Appleby Matthews of the Birmingham Police Band conducted; my task was to find a first-class chamber-orchestra to play the score, which contained very important parts for the oboe and cor anglais. Léon Goossens happened to be free, except for his Philharmonic engagement, and I snapped him up at once, being careful at the same time to secure a reliable deputy for him. His brilliant and expressive playing was one of the things that made the opera successful in London; the two Royal Princesses attended regularly and the "Hour" gradually became an institution in metropolitan music.

My fingers were itching to conduct it, but I did not get a chance until 1932, when Sir Barry revived it at the Queen's Theatre. For the first time it was equipped with an orchestra of the proper size, although we had to dig into the foundations of the theatre to make room, and when I entered the orchestra through a trap-door the 'cellists had to replace the door and sit upon it to play.

I looked after most of Sir Barry's music, and this included the Malvern Festival, for which I arranged and scored the music for Fielding's *Tom Thumb the Great*, some of which was by Arne. It was received at the Festival with roars of delight, but when reproduced at Birmingham later on, failed to attract and did not amuse very much the people who did come in. The only thing that they really laughed at was when a wooden udder, imperfectly fitted by H. K. Ayliff who made the cow, dropped off during its entrance and the hinder part of the cow (now a London director) had to sing his part in the duet holding the lactic quadriceps in his hand.

Many of Bernard Shaw's most successful plays were produced at Malvern, and I wrote what really incidental music was required. He was, of course, such a great centre of attraction for visitors that it was difficult to get him by himself; when I did, I always tried to talk music to him, remembering that he was once a music critic. He was, like myself, a lover of Mozart, and once I very nearly trapped him into saying that Mozartian simplicity made him easy to understand, but he just balked at the open ditch. But what a brilliant and informed talker he was, disseminating knowledge and culture in a soft Irish brogue and dissecting counter-argument with the skill of a surgeon.

One morning he invited me to breakfast, and the night before I went to bed without supper so that I would be up in time with an appetite. But Shaw took a constitutional before his breakfast and marched me up the Beacon at nine miles an hour, laughing heartily when I paused half-way to admire the view. "I thought ye were a mountaineer," he said, and I could only point to my expanded waist-line in self-defence. He himself was tremendously fit for a man of his age.

When Sir Barry produced *The Apple Cart* at Malvern, all the critics were flown over from London, among them my old friend Hannen Swaffer, who, running true to grain, gave the play a very bad notice. Swaff's solitary "bird" was shown to Shaw, who was expected to be indignant and asked if he had anything to say. "Not a word," said G.B.S., "but fancy sending Swaffer to criticize an intellectual play like *The Apple Cart* and paying his fare by aeroplane too!"

In his play *Too True To Be Good* Shaw took a look over the

fence into the next world, but the New Theatre patrons would not tip up 12s 6d to find out what he thought about it. Shaw was not in the least daunted and blamed the failure on to the cast, all of whom were old friends and servants. Personally, I liked *Back to Methuselah* best of his plays, with its queer visions of present-day life. It took three days to perform, and Shaw remarked that its one hundredth performance would very nearly coincide with its anniversary, both of which events he looked forward to with the utmost confidence.

When *Yellow Sands* was produced at the Haymarket in 1926, I had to write three or four songs which occurred in the action of Eden Philpotts' play. One of them, about two Devonshire lovers, was to be sung by Cedric Hardwicke, and though I did not much like the "whimsy" words, I set to work to compose a pleasant little song with a simple accompaniment for Sir Cedric to play upon the piano. Ayliff, the producer, would have none of it. "That's not what I want," he roared, "it might have been written by Norman O'Neill." "And a very good model, too," said I. "Norman O'Neill is alive," said Ayliff, "and if I wanted that kind of song I could have asked him to write it. I want a song that might have been printed in *The News of the World* to be sung in the village pub."

Highly indignant, I made an awful contraption of all the sentimental ballad-clichés I could remember, which to my great disgust was accepted by everybody with rapture. What is worse, when they made the film of *Yellow Sands*, they turned this awful tripe into a theme song and spread it all over the play like jam on the school-treat bread and butter.

Sir Barry made a sensation in London in 1925 with his *Hamlet in Plus-fours*, as it was nicknamed, though I can't say I was impressed with this present-day setting of Shakespeare's masterpiece. I wrote some music, very much against the grain, to correspond with the décor, including the first original "Charleston" ever heard in this country for the King's up-springing, and a Gigue of Handel's scored for a small dance band. Some of the sentimental music was distantly derived from *Tristan und Isolde*, the Danish National Anthem was jazzed up, and altogether it is a wonder that we were not all struck by lightning. It is a strange fact that when the production was leased to the *Volksoper* in Vienna, the management liked the music and had copies made without even asking my permission. The score was used afterwards for the ordinary Elizabethan production, so I am afraid there must have been someone in authority a little deficient in sense of humour.

Another interesting production of Sir Barry's was *The Marvellous History of Saint Bernard*, a mediaeval play adapted by him for the Kingsway in 1926. The players strolled about all over the theatre and the musicians were hidden behind a huge rock in the orchestra pit. The "orchestra" consisted of two oboes, two bassoons, harp and timpani, all Philharmonic players; you will not need telling who was the principal. There was an excellent little choir and, if I may say so, the music was highly praised, this being due more to the exquisite rendering of it than to any intrinsic value in the score itself.

Sir Barry later found a job after his own heart at the Shakespeare Memorial Theatre, Stratford-upon-Avon. When I went up to Stratford to compose the scores for *Macbeth* and *The Taming of the Shrew*, I found him happily working with Anthony Quayle and John Gielgud, who was one of his earliest *protégés* at the Regent Theatre. I tried to interest him in my new comic operetta *The 'Orse* but his mind was set on higher things.

CHAPTER XXIV

Richard Tauber and Anny Ahlers

★

I HAD NEVER regarded Hannen Swaffer as a particular friend of mine, and most actors, I think, disliked him because he was wont to intrude into a paean of praise with a croak of disapproval. I was therefore much astonished when he walked down through the Hippodrome stalls after the first act of *The Maid of the Mountains*, one night in 1931, with a pinch of snuff in his left hand, while with the other he patted me on the shoulder and said, "Ernest, let me introduce you to Bertie Scott."

I was a little annoyed because I had no idea who Mr. Scott was, but "Swaff", having disposed of the snuff, continued: "He is going to bring over the great German tenor, Richard Tauber, and that demands a strong hand at the musical helm. I have told him you are the one man in London for the job, and if you want it you can talk to him yourself." With that he disappeared in the direction of the Bar, and I told Mr. Scott that nothing would give me greater pleasure if the music (loftily) was up to my standard. Scott said: "It is a Chinese operetta by Leháh called *The Land of Smiles* which he wrote specially for Tauber." "I should love it," said I, and made an appointment for the morning.

We soon fixed up the business details; the opera was, at first, designed for His Majesty's Theatre, but Scott was able eventually to get Drury Lane, with its much larger auditorium. I engaged an orchestra of thirty-six, containing some of the best players in the country, and a first-rate chorus, and we proceeded to cast and rehearse the play with that good tenor, Robert Naylor, as a stand-in for Tauber. He was to come over at the last minute, when everything was ready, and meanwhile was trying to master what he called "zese dialogs" in English. When the day came, I went down to Dover with Scott to meet the great man, and waited on the pier for his arrival. When the boat came in the first to disembark was King Alfonso of Spain, who had just abdicated from the throne, and all the way up to London there were Spanish flags out in his honour. Richard thought the flags were a personal welcome for him, and was very pleased thereat.

He stalked into Drury Lane Theatre the next morning, and we played the music through for him. "Excellent orchestra, excellent," he said. "Magnificent playing, but you need more strings. Is it possible to get more players of this quality?"

"Rather," said I, "if Mr. Scott will pay the bill."

"Why, of course," said Richard, "you will, Bertie, won't you?"

"Yes," said Scott, a little ruefully. "How many?"

"Let me see," said Tauber, "six more fiddles, two more violas, another 'cello, and another double-bass—no—I think eight more fiddles."

I engaged the players before Scott had time to change his mind, and we finished up with a really magnificent body of troops.

Tauber had great difficulty with the "dialogs" and insisted on singing in German. I shall never forget that first night. The great audience listened with appreciation to the opening music, waiting for the great man's appearance on the stage. When he entered, there was a gasp of surprise. Instead of the musical comedy hero they expected here was a little stout lame man, with a monocle in one eye. The audience was breathless while he sang in that glorious tenor voice the opening song, "Always Smiling". They had never heard singing like that in a light opera in this country, and he limped his way through the *Tauberlied*, as Lehár called it. "You are my Heart's Delight".

We could have taken twenty encores; we did take six, and Tauber, the orchestra and I improvised a different way of singing it each time. It was a real triumph, and we all settled down comfortably for a year's run. But the next night Tauber was hoarse, and the third performance was practically an orchestral recital with Tauber speaking the words painfully. On the fourth night we had Robert Naylor on in his place, and good man as he is, he could not be expected to draw as Tauber had done. Scott, however, had made a very shrewd deal with an insurance company, and we proceeded to enjoy our own performances to half empty houses for some weeks at the expense of the Prudential. When Tauber returned, I thought his voice was impaired, but the booking office became busy again and it was arranged for Lehár to come over and conduct a performance himself to give the show a fresh fillip.

Some people expected a change in the performance; but they were disappointed, as the composer, a man of engaging personality, possessed of continental manners, requested everybody to continue without change. He was delighted with the singing and playing, he said, though he asked me to sit beside him in the pit to give him the tip when the cues came. "You in the orchestra shall sit and my leg shall pull," said he, "when you to Vienna shall come, I in the pit shall sit and your leg shall pull." Lehár gave me a large bronze medal of himself in a round white box upon which was written "To my friend and colleague, Ernest Irving, with gratitude." I was very proud of this and it has a top spot in my daughter Echo's collection.

Tauber came over again later with his German company to play the original version of *Lilac Time—Dreimäderlhaus*, and I conducted. I thought it better musically than the English production, but a Schubert-loving critic, Richard Capell, disliked Tauber's liberties, gave it a slating, and the visit ended in a "flop".

Caricature of Richard Tauber by S. Wolkowicka.

I met Tauber again in the streets of Salzburg with his charming wife, Diana Napier. He invited us to partake of *Apfelstrüdel* and we had a most pleasant re-union. Diana warned us not to be too ready to anticipate Richard in paying the bill and when the waiter came there was a four-bar pause. "Richard!" snapped Diana, peremptorily tapping him on the wrist, and all was well.

Tauber was the only man whom I ever saw knock Sir Thomas Beecham out flat. He was playing at Covent Garden in Smetana's *The Bartered Bride* and Beecham was conducting. Our lively baronet took one of the numbers much faster than the singers liked it, and one of them remonstrated, saying that Smetana's was well known to have adopted a much slower tempo. "Smetana, I regret to say," said Sir Thomas, "is dead; I happen to be musical director here," and he proceeded to take the number a little faster than before with the result that it went to pieces altogether. There was an ominous pause, then Tauber, doffing his three-cornered hat and clasping it to his breast, advanced down stage and faced Sir Thomas who was now standing on the rostrum bristling with anger.

"Yes, Herr Tauber, what is it?"

"You must be patient, Sir Thomas," said the tenor softly, "we have been singing it wrong for so many years that it will take us a few minutes to put it right."

"Next number," said Sir Thomas.

Bertie Scott's next venture was a musical play with music by Millöcker called *The Dubarry*, in which he contemplated starring Ghita Alpar, the famous Austrian soprano. With this in view he leased His Majesty's Theatre—this was in 1932—and engaged me and a large company which included Heddle Nash, the famous tenor. But something went wrong with the contract and no prima donna turned up to the rehearsal. Some time before that Eduard Künneuke, when I was conducting his *Riki-Tiki* at the Gaiety, had played to me an operetta on the subject of Lord Nelson and Lady Hamilton, and told me of a beautiful red-headed German girl who was magnificent in the title role, though strictly speaking, he said, she could not sing. This operetta was eventually performed in England with another star, but Jack Hulbert tried to turn it into a musical comedy and in the process ruined it.

One afternoon I was rehearsing the chorus of *The Dubarry* on the stage of the Gaiety Theatre when I became conscious of a presence. Turning round, I saw sitting on the end of a form a beautiful red-haired girl, patiently waiting till we had an interval. I knew instinctively and at once who it was, though I had had no warning whatever, and went up to her, offering my hand, and said, "You are Anny Ahlers." "Ja," said she, "'ow you know?" I suppose it was Künneke's vivid description, but I have never seen anybody quite like Anny. Her personality was unique and overwhelming.

She had a loud raucous singing voice, but we kept that a secret while she learned to speak the English dialogue. The day came when a decision had to be made, and at the first rehearsal with the orchestra I said to Anny, "Don't sing, act the scene, speak the words, sing a note or two here and there but no top ones, and leave the rest to us." I then trained the musicians in twenty different variations of "I Give My Heart", so that artist and orchestra became united in emotional expression.

London rose to Anny. In all my sixty years I have never seen such a triumph. She did not attempt to use her singing voice but treated the orchestral background most intelligently as a support and "booster". Each night's performance was a little different from the one before.

Then came the tragedy and the hand of fate struck poor Anny down. Driven mad by an unhappy love affair, she threw herself out of her window in Duchess Street to death on the pavement. There was a crowded memorial service at St. Paul's, Covent Garden, and later on her ashes were interred at a church at Shipley in Sussex. The whole of the company with the orchestra of forty went down, and the little stone church was filled with music. A friend of mine, out walking, was astonished to hear what sounded like a symphony orchestra coming from the church, and peeped in to see that it really was a symphony orchestra playing a movement of Brahms' Second Symphony. Elgar's "Nimrod" and Walford Davies' "Solemn Melody" had been suggested, but Brahms had painted a recognizable picture of that beautiful child-like sensitive nature extinguished in such untimely misfortune, and so I chose his music to play her exit.

CHAPTER XXV

Sydney Carroll and the Farjeons

★

IT WAS THROUGH Basil Dean that I first made contact with Sydney Carroll, who had given up a career as dramatic critic for what I imagine is a much more entertaining way of earning a living, that of an impresario. Carroll and Dean had hatched a conspiracy. Both being lovers of music, and neither knowing anything whatever about it, they had conceived the idea of reproducing Humperdinck's opera *Hansel and Gretel*, but on a smaller scale and in an ordinary theatre, the Cambridge, in 1933. The startling thing about it was that one, or both of them, had cast the part of Hansel, a contralto, for Leslie French. Leslie is a well known and very good Shakespearean actor and his Ariel is famous, but he has a thin, weak little voice which —whatever you call it, and I have heard it called many things —is certainly not contralto. The venture was backed, I understand, by a man who was interested in a young conductor and it is sad to relate that Humperdinck's score proved too much for him, as indeed it must for any novice.

My job was to reduce the score and make it playable on a band of about quarter Covent Garden size; not only because of the cost but because the Cambridge Theatre orchestra pit would only hold twenty-two players and was walled-in with concrete. Dean, with his eye for realism, had the idea of having real rabbits running about in the forest, and this, while providing nightly exercise for the property man in catching them, proved to balance the eccentricity of the casting.

My late assistant at Drury Lane and His Majesty's Theatre, Richard Austin, took the place of the novice at the conductor's rostrum: he made a fine job of it, and it started him on a career which sees him now in the front rank of British conductors. The concentrated essence of Humperdinck sounded quite reasonably good, but it is not a job I would undertake again—unless I needed the money as much as I did then.

The next time I heard from Sydney Carroll was in 1936 at a trade show of a film which I was conducting at the Piccadilly Theatre. I received a message that Carroll and his lady stage manager were waiting to see me in the inn on the other side of Denman Street, and, appearing there as soon as possible, I found Sydney in great trouble.

He was presenting a Victorian operetta by Herbert and Eleanor Farjeon called *The Two Bouquets*, for which Eleanor had picked out of her mother's song books some forty Victorian airs to embellish the action of the play. Now, in spite of popular fancy, airs do not leap out of mother's song book prepared for incorporation in the score of an opera and Herman Finck, who had undertaken the task of collating, arranging and orchestrating them, was called away to a bigger production. *The Two Bouquets* was cast and had been rehearsing a week at the Ambassadors' Theatre, and I remarked to Sydney: "It looks to me as if you are either short of time or money." He replied, "Both my lad." I said, "Well, let me read the book and I will see what I can do." A very few pages of Herbert Farjeon's witty dialogue convinced me it was worth while and the next morning I telephoned Sydney and told him that I would undertake the job, but that it would be a miracle if I could get through it in the two weeks available. There was to be a "full symphony orchestra" of eight players to suit the small theatre, and I demanded—and, after a long fight, extracted—a ninth. It was a very lucky adventure, as it ran for six months at the Ambassadors' and then went to the Garrick Theatre, and has recently been revived with great success at the St. Martin's and Piccadilly theatres. I got a lot of personal kudos and made great friends with the two Farjeons.

Later on, in 1938, we collaborated in another opera called *An Elephant in Arcady*. In this case I came earlier upon the scene and was able to take part in the selection of the music, for which Eleanor had drawn largely upon the two Scarlattis and their compatriots, and I was able to introduce many of the lesser works of Mozart. The production was run as a sort of republic. My score was for seventeen players this time, and, like those in *The Two Bouquets*, they were all virtuosi. The book was amusing and the lyrics brilliant light verse. It was splendidly cast with Irene Eisinger, Frederick Ranalow, Geoffrey Dunn, Eric Starling, and Edmund Donlevy and other good singers; they all loved the show which reached, I think, an artistic level equal to anything which could be seen in London at that time.

The production was not so good. I thought the opening scene looked like a Yorkshire railway station. One of the songs was set to that immortal melody, the slow movement of Mozart's Clarinet Concerto. The introduction to the scene was played by a clarinet—Charles Draper, probably the finest classical player in the world—and repeated by the voice. At a rehearsal the singer said, "And what am I supposed to do during the sixteen bars of the clarinet solo? Do I just walk about and look at the flowers?" Replied the producer: "If I were you I should sit down and listen to Mr. Draper, and, when he has finished, see if you can sing it as well as he has played it." This was not quite fair as, after all, Mozart wrote it for the clarinet and not for the voice.

An Elephant in Arcady had quite a respectable run at the Kingsway and the Savoy theatres, but the railway strike brought it to an end. It was always, I am afraid, a little bit above the tastes of the ordinary theatre-goer. I was engaged upon another pastiche with Herbert Farjeon, employing Handel's music, which was smashed by his untimely death.

1886

1947

The author and Sir Thomas Beecham

Carroll came back with another crusade in 1938. He had for some time run a summer season of plays in the open air in Regent's Park, and he now hatched the idea of adding opera (and Mozart at that), asking me to direct it. He proposed to use the Webber-Douglas Company, an organisation which for years had studied and performed opera under the direction of that talented conductor Amherst Webber and Johnstone Douglas, the singer. They were perfectly organised and rehearsed to the last quaver, which was very lucky for me, as you will hear. Carroll added to the cast some well-known singers, including Dennis Noble and Winifred Lawson. The company performed usually with two pianos instead of an orchestra, and they had a lady conductor who was engaged as my deputy. I believe she was very good, but, I regret to say, I never gave her a chance.

We made the London County Council, to the great disgust of the green keeper, dig a trench for the orchestra pit, in front of the greensward stage, for you cannot hide a Mozart orchestra of thirty-five behind the laurel bushes. Open air acoustics were bound to be difficult, but Carroll arranged a set of microphones with speakers for the big arena, in case the summer breezes blew the other way.

On the first night there was a thunderstorm. The orchestra pit looked like the Findhorn at Lossiemouth; my second oboe was nearly drowned in trying to recover his reed from the brown flood, and we had to repair to a tent which the Regent's Park company use for such emergencies. That first performance was one of the toughest engagements I have ever fought. The orchestra piled up in a pyramid near the pit stalls with the rain driving through openings in the canvas, thirty yards away from the singers, twelve rows of stalls between my desk and the voices—I could not hear a note. The rain poured down the back of my neck from a devilishly accurate little hole in the roof and I had to depend upon the singers answering to the smallest fluctuations in my beat and rendering the music as rehearsed. To this demand they rose most nobly, and to this day my heart bursts with gratitude to Amherst Webber and Johnstone Douglas for the meticulous way in which they had rehearsed their company.

CHAPTER XXVI

Basil Dean and Beecham

★

To RETURN TO Basil Dean and less psychic experiences. Sometime before, I had been called in by Sir Alfred Butt to re-set the music to *The Two Little Vagabonds* at the Empire, and this led to an engagement to fix three or four feature films which I did with varying success.

When talking films came in, I was associated in an experiment at the Bushey studio of Professor Herkomer with William Wilson, the producer of *The Lilac Domino*. Believe it or not, we started by trying to make an opera—Gounod's *Romeo and Juliet*—and the idea was to make synchronised gramophone discs by recording through an insulated glass window. Wilson had very little backing, so I rescored Gounod for a band of twelve, which varied from day to day as we had some trouble with the Musicians Union. Naturally this cheeky venture was a failure, but I learnt a good deal that was useful about synchronised sound recording, and when Dean asked me to join him in making a sound film I was delighted to accept.

He had formed a company with Sir Gerald du Maurier called Associated Talking Pictures. The first film was Galsworthy's *Escape*, and it was made at Beaconsfield Studios. One scene was shot in Hyde Park at night and was really a grand "do". Dean had hired for me the band of the Welsh Guards with Major Andrew Harris to conduct it, and he had ensnared half fashionable London to act as the crowd, thus giving him a thousand extras free. I could tell many amusing stories of that night, but

I will only say that all the sound we recorded was unusual because it was mixed with the noise of the dynamos. Early in the morning, just as the nursemaids began to come into Hyde Park, Dean tried to get a record of some hunting songs which I had arranged, but a thrush sat on our microphone, carolling lustily, and thwarting all his efforts. Time pressed and he got angry, picked up a chunk of wood, hove it at the bird, missed it, and shattered the microphone. This concluded a night packed with adventure.

Escape was finished at Beaconsfield, where the music had to be post-synchronised against time, as money was limited and musicians are expensive. The film, in spite of its shortcomings, was a good one and deserved its success.

The company then acquired its studios at Ealing to continue its work. Dean appointed me music director and I screwed my brass plate on to the music room door, where it remained until May 1st, 1953, when it was transferred to the bedroom in which I write.

The years at Ealing with Dean were all exciting, because all the time we were learning something new about this kaleidoscopic art which changes its aim and method week by week. We dealt with Gracie Fields and established her as a film star, George Formby, Will Hay, Tommy Trinder, Jack Warner, and others, and most of our films were both good and successful. Dean was a little pinched for money and mean in his music budgets. I had to make do with small orchestras, but I saw to it that they contained the very best players in England.

When we did the Mozart film *Whom the Gods Love*, we had a very jolly trip to Salzburg where we met Bernhard Paumgartner of the *Mozarteum*, who knows everything about the great man from the cradle to the grave. We visited the *Geburtshaus* and I was invited to play on Mozart's little klavier which stood in the corner.

I naturally demurred; all the greatest pianists in the world had touched those keys and their names are recorded in a book.

I was over-persuaded, however, thought for a moment, and then began to play from memory a lovely little Sonata in A major; a limpid and simple piece of masterwork. When I finished, everybody laughed and I was a little nettled. I said, "I know I did not play it well, but was it as bad as all that?" "No," said Paumgartner with a smile, "but the strange thing is that everybody who sits down to that instrument plays that tune and their names are ticked off in red, as you see in the book." No doubt I selected it because it was easy, but there must be some aura about the instrument which made Liszt and Schnabel select it too.

While in Salzburg we made several excursions, amongst them a visit to Berchtesgaden, which is the last visa in that passport of mine. I remember standing outside the post office there and laughing at an enormous life-size photograph of Adolf Hitler—it was so enlarged that the face was an area of large pimples—to the great disapproval of the Postmaster. He suddenly stiffened to attention and there whirled past us, two yards away, the great Fuehrer in a great Mercedes with three generals in full uniform, all sitting bolt upright on their way to a holiday at Hitler's country house. It was a startling episode and the only time I saw him at close quarters.

From Salzburg I brought back several little knick-knacks, including a broad-brimmed felt hat of a peculiarly virulent bright green. Passing the Customs, I declared my dutiable goods. "Anything else?" asked the Inspector. "Well, there's this," I said, and handed him my green hat. He took it from me, turned back the leather band inside, and there, in gold letters, was stamped "Made in Birmingham". With a smile, he replaced it on my head. Nevertheless, that hat was very useful; every time I wore it people nudged one another and smiled. When I walked into a recording session everybody was grinning, and, may I ask, what better way is there to start a day's work than to have every face with a smile on it? Five years ago I gave it to a friend who tells me he used it in Australia with great effect.

Back at Ealing, I suggested to Dean that I should try to interest Sir Thomas Beecham in a film and get him to conduct the operatic parts. I received permission and brought off a coup, but, said Sir Thomas, you cannot show an opera like *The Magic Flute* with a lot of snippets. Neither, said Dean, can I stop and perform a four-hour opera in its entirety, as a film cannot last longer than ninety minutes. The work Beecham did do, however, was superlatively good, though his comments on film methods with music were fierce and free. A photograph of him contemplating an empty dust-bin with me is reproduced in this book; I will not quote his remarks to me, except to say that they suggested a very comprehensive list of various works with which the utensil might be filled to the world's benefit.

There are hundreds of "funny" stories about Sir Thomas, but I will restrain myself, and give below only two which I think may be more or less unknown.

The first concerns Chaliapin, the great Russian bass. He had, as everybody knows, a magnificent voice which nobody admired more than he did, and when he struck a high or low note with particular sonority he had a habit of pausing upon it in sheer admiration. At morning rehearsals—*Boris Godunov* I think it was—the singer found himself in fine fettle, continually imposing pauses and *rallentandi* upon the impatient conductor. When at last he went off the stage, he found a band playing in the wings and started to conduct them, turning their allegro into an andante. Beecham sighed and quietly closed his score and put down his baton. "Ladies and gentlemen," he said, "this rehearsal began a long time ago in the early morning. It has dragged itself along for many hours during which it has become slower, and slower, and slower, in fact I think (stepping off the rostrum) I may confidently say that it has stopped altogether." The orchestra of course melted away with alacrity. When Chaliapin finished his little piece he was surprised at the unexpected silence. He poked his head out of the wings, discovered the pit to be empty, and made some remarks in Russian; what they were I cannot tell you, as I do not speak Russian.

The other story, which I personally like very much, is of Bristol Cathedral, where at a festival Sir Thomas was conducting several oratorios, including *Messiah*. He had touched up the orchestration for this and added a third trumpet part which was played by Solomon, in his day the best trumpeter in England. At the rehearsal Solomon was missing from his desk, and Sir Thomas sent a scout round to his room, to find that he had left early and had gone to look at the shops. The scout eventually found Solomon with his nose against a jeweller's window and told him that Sir Thomas wanted him at once. The old trumpeter had thought that another oratorio was being rehearsed, but he rushed home for his trumpet and got to the Cathedral to find the rehearsal finished and everyone gone.

At the performance, with all the dignitaries of the Diocese in full array, he found himself behind a pillar, and, anxious to make amends when his entrance came, popped his head and trumpet out, and triumphantly came in—a bar too soon! Sir Thomas, conducting at the lectern in cassock and surplice, turned wearily to the nearest listener, who happened to be the Dean, and remarked "There's that ——— Wandering Jew again!"

As I said, I could fill a book with stories of Sir Thomas, but I will not say any more of this side of him because there are people who think of him as a sort of musical clown. I advise them to have another think. Here is an erudite scholar, a perfect artist and a passionate lover of music, at his peak a genius; a generous employer, a charming companion and a perfect host. He has done more for music in this country than any man living—I was going to say "or dead", when just in time I remembered Handel.

It was Beecham's work for *The Magic Flute* that prompted this digression (Beecham is liable to provide digressions). But to return. Mozart, at that time, was caviare to the film public. For the Manchester trade show, I engaged the Hallé Orchestra, and we played bits of Mozart before and after the presentation. There was a buffet for refreshment in one of the bars, and there I found a little exhibitor from Bedford Leigh cornered by an enormous man we employed as selling agent.

Agent: "So you don't like Moz-zart, don't you?"
Exhibitor: "NO I DON'T."
Agent: "Well, No *Moz-zart—No Griecie Fields.*"
Exhibitor: "Well, I'll pay for it, but I daresen't show it, they would throw bricks through the screen."

Dean's work both for the screen and the stage was always a little in front of his time, and I personally think was very much under-valued. He had a flair for finding talented assistants—I was a shining example!—but when he asked their advice, he very seldom took it. He knew nothing about music, but loved it, and, somehow or other, selected the best to love. His idea of having Delius to write the music for that blood-thirsty play *Hassan* was fantastically wrong but successful. He practically discovered Benjamin Britten and gave him half the score for *Johnson Over Jordan* to do—to my great disgust, as I had expected, and indeed contracted, to do it all. His first act was very brittle and untheatrical but he finished the play with a terrific brass statement of the Dies Irae, with a great smite on the largest gong in London when Johnson stepped off this world into the Infinite. It was thrilling, not to say blood-curdling, and fully made up for the lack of theatricality in his first act.

When the Second World War started, Dean and Seymour Hicks were entrusted with the formation of E.N.S.A. and set up their offices in Drury Lane Theatre, which had been put out of action by a bomb. They called me in and appointed me music director, but I couldn't put up my brass plate as Herman Finck had left his on his door, and I was allotted a room underneath the stage with no air and very little furniture. Dean is writing a book himself about E.N.S.A., so I will not continue with its history except to remark that it soon grew to such a size as to demand a whole-time musical head and I was forced to hand it over to my assistant James Walker.

There is one story about E.N.S.A. which I must tell. There was a conference one day between Hicks, Dean, and two B.B.C. representatives in which a famous novelist in a milk-white suit was planning a programme. During a session he continually mispronounced Thucydides, finishing it off with 'dy-des'." Nobody turned a hair and I heard afterwards that the B.B.C. men mistook our politeness for ignorance of the classics. Afterwards the novelist went to reclaim a book he had left with my secretary. "Let me see," said she, "this is the one, I think, by General I-ron-si-des." "Ironsides, my dear," said the novelist, "Ironsides", and departed down the stairs with a hearty laugh.

Basil Dean had a wonderful grasp of detail, in fact I think he sometimes put his nose too close to the window. He had some failures, it is true, but he had some great successes as well. I should like to see him make a film of *Hassan* with somebody else's music. I have to thank him for the job which has enabled me to end my days in comfort. He once nearly sacked me, and I once nearly told him to go to the devil, but luckily for both of us, especially me, temperatures did not reach flash point.

CHAPTER XXVII

Mona Inglesby and "International Ballet"

★

I WAS FIRST brought into contact with the amiable and mercurial personality of Mona Inglesby, mainspring and prima ballerina assoluta of the International Ballet, by her music director, Julian Clifford, who commissioned me to score a ballet for her based on Shakespeare's *Twelfth Night* fitted to music by Grieg. I thought it most unfitted, and could not see what Grieg had to do with Shakespeare, or either of them with the ballet, but it was a new adventure, and gave me the chance to push in the songs I had written for Sir Oswald Stoll's production of the play, in which they were sung by Laidman Brown. Leslie French was to play Feste in the ballet; he is not much of a singer, as I have said before, and has a small light voice, but, being highly intelligent and an accomplished artist, he knew exactly how to "put over" these songs. Strange to say, *Twelfth Night* in dumb show, or as one critic put it in "leg-endary form", was very successful, and I made a little interlude for Leslie of some other Shakespearean songs which he exploited to the obvious approval of the ballet audiences. I remember that Algeranoff made an impressive Malvolio; Mona herself played Viola.

All this seemed very strange and new, and when I was asked to score a 'Divertissement" called *Aurora's Wedding*—an extract from Tchaikowsky—and to collaborate with Frederic

Austin in arranging *Swan Lake* for the International's small orchestra (then only seventeen) I readily complied. Then Mona invited me to go down occasionally to the ballet as a "guest conductor".

Now, if you are bold enough to want to conduct ballet at all, it is certainly best, if you can arrange it, to start as a guest. The rules of hospitality entitle you to make experiments and mistakes, and you are starred on the bills and programmes without regard to your ability. I had some experience with Massine and Karsavina at the Empire and had made some arrangements for the Rambert and Jooss Ballets, but this was my first real excursion down the rabbit-hole into Wonderland, where everything, music, dancers, and audiences, was fantastic, and the conductor's art had to be mastered all over again.

One cannot learn to swim without going into the water, and the first bit of empirical knowledge I acquired was this. When the dancer is in extra-good form, or the audience extra-large and enthusiastic, you would expect the music to liven up to correspond and the tempo to quicken in feeding the excitement. Not so, the jumps are higher and the leaps are longer; the dancer takes more time in the air, and you've just got to wait till she comes down, as the audience can both see and hear the impact. The foot-work, on the contrary, may be a shade quicker, and the result is a rubato that is on the whole considerably slower than usual. Other measures have to be adopted by the conductor to keep the excitement alive, and these I propose to keep a trade secret, merely observing that they involve the understanding collaboration of the orchestra, and considerable concentration by everybody. I stipulated with "Jimmy" Inglesby, the shrewd and kindly impresario, for not less than six first violins when I conducted, stealing a march, I'm afraid, on the regular man, and altogether had a high time picking up the technical wrinkles of this very intricate branch of musical art. I think it is the most difficult job I have ever had, excepting only that of conducting a music hall variety programme, which needs a wizard.

One day Mona had the idea of dancing *Coppélia* and took me along to see the Sadlers Wells performance. It struck me that the score sounded thin, as if they had just left out the parts for which they had no players in the orchestra. As ours was smaller still, it was obviously a matter for transcription rather than condensation, and I started to search the British Museum and the other London music libraries for a copy of the original full score. We drew blank, there *is* no original full score, and a great deal of the orchestration appears to have been done by other hands than those of a Delibes, in fact some of it in the last-minute throes of production seems to have been scored straight into parts! So we had to rely on the cues in the printed piano score, and that gave me a pretty free hand. This brought some criticism, as you may read elsewhere, from the ballet Pressmen, but not many of them know much about music anyway, and the "adaptation" was an unquestionable success; it has been played a thousand times, and borrowed by the B.B.C. for use on television. In the score I paid particular attention to strengthening the little dramatic bits, and here I was on firm ground.

One of the queer things a ballet conductor has to get used to, is "taking a curtain" with the dancers after the "floral offerings" have been handed up. The prima ballerina beckons him on, he bows to right and left and charges down-stage in the line, skipping the floral barrier with what agility he can command. Successfully over, he is left alone to indicate his gratitude to the orchestra and the audience. The line skips down again to pick him up, and he retires, bowing, with them, and I can tell you that the backward skip over the bouquets requires finesse for a middle-aged man of gouty tendency.

On the first night at the Savoy in 1944 the last curtain was taken by Sergei Sergareff, that encyclopaedic little Russian who learnt his job with the Czar's Imperial Ballet and who now produced all Mona's ballets. The old man skipped down in the line and was left on the floats to a hurricane of applause, which he did nothing to subdue; but when it finished he started a speech of thanks in broken English. It went on for five minutes, ten—fifteen. Some of the less ardent "fans" drifted away, and the cabmen poked their noses into the theatre to see what was going on. At last, on Mona's orders, I strode over the flowers, and, tapping him on the shoulder, led him upstage to much applause and friendly laughter, and while his back was turned, got the fireproof curtain down. He had, I am sure, plenty more to say; a great artist completely master of his job. His note-books, Mona tells me, contain diagrams of every step and stage grouping in all the classical ballets and he would allow no deviations by anybody.

During the next year there were all sorts of little happenings, including a small ballet I wrote myself for Mona, Leslie French, and Algeranoff called *Adam and Eve*. I don't think it can have been very good, it was poorly rehearsed, badly played; performed two or three times somewhere in Yorkshire and buried. "Jimmy" paid up (perhaps it wasn't quite so bad as all that, and may some day be disinterred). But I think the main reason for dropping it may have been Mona's big new idea for Leslie French, *Everyman* set to the music—believe it or not—of Richard Strauss's Symphonic Poems—*Till Eulenspiegel's Merry Pranks, Don Juan* and *Tod und Verklarung*.

It did not need a hostile Pressman to wonder what Till could have to do with Everyman, but Mona was set upon it, and the next step was to get Strauss's permission to perform the outrage. Novello's got through somehow or other to him in Vienna and he said we could do anything that would popularize his music in this country. He stipulated, however, that the existing "condensed" scores should be scrapped, and that I should, in person, make the new orchestrations for a band of thirty, up to which level we had screwed the groaning "Jimmy". This was a *hell* of a job—one flute and two horns! It had always to be played at the end of a programme and the wretched hornplayers, representing six and a trombone, were completely exhausted and excused the National Anthem. It was really an outrageous thing to do, though it sounded surprisingly like the original, in fact I was once publicly congratulated in the middle of supper at a Manchester hotel by no less an authority than Sir Malcolm Sargent— who had just heard it and walked right across a large room to speak the words of praise! This was no guest conductor's job, and I engaged Wynn Reeves to conduct it. Wynn, who was leader at the Opera, had played the works under all the great conductors and knew the scores inside out. He is a very fine conductor himself and so my contraption got the best possible showing at the Adelphi.

The critics were fierce. That erudite musician, Mr. Frank Howes of *The Times*, said that it was an outrage thus to maltreat Strauss just because he was an alien enemy unable to protest. Here I thought I had him, and Dr. Aber of Novello's produced Strauss's letters, which were printed in *The Times*. But we couldn't refute the main gravamen that Till and Everyman were worlds apart; and here I may remark, for the benefit of the tyro, that it is a mistake to argue with a critic in his own paper.

Undeterred, Mona went on dancing it, Leslie went on miming it, and thousands of people paid gleefully to see it, which encouraged them both to another adventure which turned out badly for similar reasons.

Leslie wanted to play *Comus*, and this time there was a board meeting to select the composer to be carved up. Purcell was obvious but not available, as he was being used by another company. I wanted to use Mozart's smaller and unknown pieces, such as the German dances, the divertimenti, the masonic music and suchlike, but Mona, led on by gramophone records which I could not rival, carried the day for Handel. Now Handel, like Mozart, wrote many small pieces which are undeservedly unknown to the public and suitable for a ballet, but his style is a little ponderous for Milton's poetic fantasy, in which Mona played the beetle-browed witch Coccyla. Nevertheless, I could not complain of lack of material and spent hours in the British Museum copying scores, of which I had already made a good collection for the film *The Great Mr. Handel.* I thought it was a fine production; we opened, I think, at Croydon, and afterwards came to the London Coliseum.

Once again the critics disapproved. One lady sneered (possibly remembering the film) at my "lush" harmonies; it was vain to protest that there wasn't a note in the whole ballet that was not written by Handel himself or justified by his figured basses. I think it was just too Miltonian for the Handelians, too dramatic for the ballet fans, and incongruous to the ordinary theatregoer, Still, it was good fun while it lasted.

I stopped "guest conducting" after Mona's third season at the Adelphi for which she had engaged two American stars. They were to open the season and wanted, I believe, to dance *Swan Lake,* which Mona had wished to reserve for herself; and *Coppélia* was chosen instead. Their tempi, and, indeed, their conception of the parts, were quite different from Sergareff's, and I rehearsed them very carefully with the orchestra, altering the markings in the orchestral parts to suit their rendering.

I was very much under the weather at this time with heart weakness and on my way to the first performance I called, not at the Cavour for a porterhouse steak, but at my doctor's for a "shot". What he injected I shall never know, but I am reliably informed that I gave the rhythms tremendous emphasis and brought the orchestra back to their original tempi. For when I reached the theatre I was informed that the new lady star had a bad sore throat (which was quite true) and that neither of them would appear!

Now half the stalls was packed with members of other ballet companies who wanted to see the Americans and had *paid for their seats,* so when a very indiscreet manager came on and broke the news, saying that Miss Inglesby had kindly agreed to dance *Coppélia* for the 1,253rd time, there was nearly a riot. There was no time to say anything to the orchestra except "Ignore the new markings and watch the beat" and off we went to as hostile an audience as Daniel had in the Lions' Den.

Next day, the Press followed suit. I remembered Pistol's lines —"Old do I wax and from my weary limbs, honour is cudgelled"—and at the end of the season handed my baton to my second-in-command James Walker, who has "wielded" it most artistically ever since. I must add in pure self-defence that when the Americans did dance *Coppélia* I conducted the performance with tremendous swank, and to the satisfaction, freely expressed, of the dancers, the Press and the public.

I still keep up my connection with the Ballet, and helped to enlarge *Aurora* into the full *Sleeping Princess* but have left Walker to conduct the tours which have been extended, with great success, to Spain and Italy.

Thank you, dear Mona, for these most enjoyable experiences.

CHAPTER XXVIII

Michael Balcon

★

WHEN BASIL DEAN left Ealing to join Seymour in the direction of Ensa, Ealing prospects looked pretty dim. I never knew or cared much about the financial side of film production, but I believe that the millionaire brothers Courtauld were behind the little producing company which was called Associated Talking Pictures. Ealing has a fine record in the production of comedy; Gracie Fields, George Formby, Will Hay and Tommy Trinder were all best-sellers. Their songs were written by our English Wardour-Street composers and the incidental music was mostly composed by me.

Dean was, I think, pinched a little in the amount he could spend upon music and I squeezed as many players out of him as I could and engaged them one at a time. In his bigger productions such as *Lorna Doone* and the Mozart film, he spread himself a little, and for the latter film I was allowed to have Sir Thomas Beecham and the London Philharmonic Orchestra. But generally we "managed" with thirty or forty and I had to be very sharp with rehearsal costs.

Michael Balcon somehow brought a different atmosphere; he also brought William Walton to write the music for *Next of Kin*, a film that we were making in association with the War Office. He was very polite in introducing Walton; I think he feared I might be jealous. This, of course, would have been ridiculous, as I had already survived the introduction of Mozart; I considered, and said so promptly, that it was a grand thing to get a composer of Walton's calibre associated with Ealing films. Afterwards we had Rawsthorne, John Ireland, Georges Auric and Ralph Vaughan Williams, not to mention Leslie Bridgewater, Gordon Jacob, John Greenwood, William Alwyn, John Addison and Benjamin Frankel.

When the London Philharmonic Orchestra became too busy, I changed over to Philharmonia, just formed by Walter Legge for H.M.V. recording. As most people know, this orchestra contains some of the best players in Europe, and I cannot be too grateful for the enthusiastic support I have received from them; as a result I think I may say without boasting that Ealing music has been equal to any film music in the world.

Michael Balcon is a living example of the fact that the head of a film studio should be a producer and not a director. Let the director do his damnedest but let him have, sitting above him, a producer in touch with the public, of culture and experienced judgement, with authority to cut, alter, cancel and expand. He must, of course, be in sympathy with his directors and encourage them with understanding and praise; but he must be ruthless when he takes up the scalpel and relentless until he is thoroughly satisfied.

Such a man is Michael Balcon, and in all my years with him I have never been cramped or stinted in my work; that is not to say that he approved or accepted everything I did, far from it, but he did understand what I was up to and recognised that spending a little more money is often the best way to avoid waste.

There are a great many more things I could say in his praise, but good manners call upon me to refrain. Now that I have retired from active participation in the work of the studio, I can only say that I congratulate the whole staff from director to clapper-boy in having such a champion in the fight with television. In the great J. Arthur Rank pool he preserved Ealing's independence, and when it ebbed emerged "bloody but unbowed". His knighthood, richly deserved, came as a recognition of the work of the whole team.

CHAPTER XXIX

Music for Shakespeare and Lesser Dramatists

★

IN THE OLD days of the theatre the incidental music in a melodrama was very prominent and, up to a point, important; one of its principal intentions was that of the fat boy "to make yer flesh creep". I received £2 for my first melodramatic score, which had to be arranged so that it could be played on any sized orchestra down to four, and the price mentioned included a full set of orchestral parts. Music was unblushingly used to brighten up an entrance, strengthen an exit, emphasise the action and wheedle a salt tear in the pathetic scenes. The string tremolo was a well used device and certain music definitely invited the audience to "give us your applause". It sometimes overdid this by interfering with the subtleties of a good class scene.

In Robert Loraine's *Cyrano de Bergerac*, for instance, there was a very juicy 'cello solo which accompanied Cyrano's great death scene. This was published and proved a best seller; any Sunday morning cycling through Surbiton you could hear it tinkling out of the drawing room windows; and yet in the play the scene never seemed to go as well as it should. I had occasion to re-score the music for broadcasting and used a viola to play the solo instead of the 'cello, so that Loraine's voice dominated the scene instead of Cedric Sharpe's 'cello. Loraine was startled by the change and asked me if I had any other suggestions. "Yes," I said, "I have one. Cut it out altogether." He was very dubious about this after all the years he had accompanied the music, but eventually took my advice and in return received a salvo of applause at the end of the scene. This instance is only given to show that it is possible to overdo "descriptive" music, which can be used most effectively if kept under proper control.

Shakespeare himself demands music here and there, and there is little doubt it was consistently used at the Globe Theatre. The tunes of the songs, of course, were older than Shakespeare and have been handed down to us with the plays, but every composer worth his salt who gets half a chance likes to put new settings to the words. I have made many settings myself and the only one that has not been used is the one of which I think most highly, *Julius Caesar*. The two I did for the Shakespeare Memorial Theatre, *Macbeth* and *The Taming of the Shrew*, were recorded and played from discs in the theatre. This enabled one to get a much greater variety of orchestral colour than can be obtained from a small "live" band but presents certain difficulties of synchronisation and prompt cue taking. In the scores I made for Colonel Stanley Bell after Norman O'Neill's death in 1934 (*Twelfth Night* and *The Merry Wives of Windsor*), I was handicapped a little because of the Colonel's insistence upon simplicity, by which he meant Victorian simplicity; in fact, the *Manchester Guardian* enquired why I had thought it worth while to write such music for *The Merry Wives*.

Henry IV at His Majesty's will be chiefly remembered because George Robey played Falstaff. Sydney Carroll gave me a first class orchestra; I had a lot of oboes with Goossens leading them and three or four percussion players, with which we made a tremendous noise for the departure of the troops at "How I wish this tavern were my drum." The music sung by Lady Mortimer to Glendower's accompaniment was "David of the White Rock", repeated by the orchestra with great effect when the two women watched through the oriel window to see their husbands depart for the Battle of Shrewsbury. For the public, Robey was the centre of attraction, in fact too much so, as everybody was waiting for him to make a "gaffe", and this made episodes like the "Honour" speech very uncomfortable to listen to. But I am bound to say that George got an enormous roar or laughter at the end of the play after the exit of Prince Henry, who, regretting the death of his old friend, had promised to have him disembowelled. "Dis-em-bowelled", said George, sitting up among the slain with eyebrows raised to semi-circle, and the laughter lasted till the end of the scene.

I have told in other chapters about the music for Barry Jackson's plus-fours *Hamlet*, and how my *Twelfth Night* music, which I don't consider to be very good, was preserved by being included in a ballet. I think most composers will agree with me that setting music to the Bard is a fascinating task and that it is a great privilege to get the opportunity of trying one's hand in public.

CHAPTER XXX

Chess in the Orchestra

★

I CANNOT REMEMBER the time when I was unable to play chess. As a very small boy I used to solve, entirely to my own satisfaction, the problems in the *Illustrated London News,* albeit that I had no idea of the functions of the pieces. It did not worry me at all that my solutions varied from the editor's and I little thought that one day I should sit in the great Howard Staunton's chair and deal with a chess mail from all over the world.

I learnt to move the pieces properly after a bloody tussle with a fellow-infant who objected to my moving the pawns backwards. Then, again, I did not think that seventy years later I should have to struggle to prevent Gilbert Harding doing the same thing in a film, though then the fight was sarcastic rather than sanguinary. I soon became quite a respectable player and invented a few unconventional devices to use in the gambits. I have told the story of meeting Mortimer, and in the provinces —when there was no mountain to climb—I used to seek out the local chess club, or, failing that, the café where chess was played, and thus became acquainted with a great many players all over the British Isles.

Not many provincial musicians played chess in those days, though I have related how the 'cellist at Blackpool nearly got me a fifth sack from Charles Cochran. In London it was different; and many tight struggles took place upon a pocket board between the numbers. I have met people who are horrified at this and cannot believe that a player can do his work properly with a chess game in his head, still less when the game is played blindfold, that is to say, without board or men.

I can only say for my part that a blind-fold game of chess is not in the least a handicap to the concentration necessary in conducting an opera, quite the reverse in fact. Brian Harley, in one of his books, makes great fun of the way the pocket boards went round during what he describes as a delightful performance of *Polly*. But Bertie Farjeon begged me to give him my word of honour that I would not play chess during the performance of *An Elephant in Arcady*. He said that he was certain that I could do both things simultaneously and successfully without sight of board or score, but that the idea horrified him. All I can say is, that it is a very good thing people cannot look into one another's brains to see what really goes on there.

Goddard of the Savage Club gave me the job of Chess Editor for the *Illustrated London News;* it was a tough task, which had to be done mostly by sitting up at night, and this made me unpopular at home, though I bought a grand new suite of furniture with the proceeds.

I entered for the big International Tournament at Westminister in 1922 and finished half-way down the first-class, won the "Referee" Correspondence Championship, have held the Ealing Silver Cup, and once beat Sultan Khan in a simultaneous display when he was champion. All this does not amount to very much, and I only bring it in to show that chess is a very useful training for the brain and not, as some people think, just a waste of time.

The lady champion, Eileen Trammer, was a clarinet player in the Sadlers Wells Orchestra. I do not know whether she played chess there, and if I did know, I should not tell; she is a strong player and well up to male first-class. I once played a blind-fold game with her during *Coppélia,* and at move eighteen she played pawn to Queen's fourth. The reply was, "What with?"—as she had exchanged the pawn earlier in Act

I, and had played quite a number of notes on her instrument afterwards.

Here is a little story about Blackburne, in his day the strongest British player and known all over Europe as the "Black Death". I was visiting Glasgow with an opera at the King's Theatre, and Blackburne was giving simultaneous displays at all the clubs. We were both staying at the house of a mutual friend at Cardross down the Clyde, and one evening, when the old man was playing twenty-four of the ladies, I dashed down in the interval to see how he was getting on. It was his interval, too, and he was sipping his "paregoric". He was winning all round, he said, but was very doubtful about his game with Miss Gibb where his Queen was uncomfortable. I took a look at the position but there appeared to be nothing wrong with it whatever. We collected him after the performance, and, surely enough, he had won every game except that one; how he lost his Queen I cannot think, but he did. Questioned on the way home, he confessed after some badgering, "Well, Miss Gibb is the Treasurer and a win may have softened her heart." He opened his little pay-packet. It had!

Tournaments were very difficult for me because adjourned games had to be finished in the evening. I managed to persuade opponents sometimes to play in my room at the theatre, and one such game in the "Budget" cup played during the run of *The Applecart* had to be abandoned as a draw. My opponent objected that when he was left alone a rat came out and stared at him and that this was too much for his nerves. I think the fact that he was a pawn down may have had something to do with it, but I had to replay the game on the street level.

I formed a little chess club in Ealing Studios which, though not strong, is very lively and sporting; now and again we get a strong player down to take us on all together.

Moral, don't believe it when any non-player mocks at chess as a waste of time.

CHAPTER XXXI

Music in the Law Courts

★

IN 1923 MY friend Frederic Austin, composer and arranger of those works of genius *The Beggar's Opera* and *Polly*, was involved in a lawsuit about the gramophone recording of the latter opera. He was negotiating a deal with Columbia but got a better offer from H.M.V. and changed over—nowadays, of course, the two companies are closely allied. Columbia, not to be dished, had another arrangement of the non-copyright tunes made by Albert Ketèlbey, the composer of "In a Monastery Garden", and Austin, not at all the man to put up with plagiarism, got H.M.V. to take it to court.

All the best known British musicians were giving evidence. The Judge was Astbury, unmusical, but reported to have a musical friend, and Austin's Counsel was Fairfax Luxmoore, K.C., afterwards the Judge. The centre bastion of the defence was Sir Frederick Bridge, organist of Westminster Abbey, and Columbia had printed an "exhibit" in which all Mr. Ketèlbey's original work was shown in red ink, and to this Sir Frederick had placed his signature of approval.

Austin, who knew and disapproved of my "chess mind", thought I could be useful, and I was. The problem was to cross-examine a great musical expert through a non-musical Counsel so that the answer could be only "yes" or "no" before a non-musical Judge who would be dead against us if any argument arose, and I wrote out in advance all the questions with this in view. In the court the great man took the oath, and gave evidence that he had superintended the "Exhibit" and agreed with its statements. Luxmoore, cross-examining, said the court was bound to take great notice of Sir Frederick's evidence, that he didn't wish to trap him in any way, and after a little legal skirmishing came to the point:—

"You have signed these examples, Sir Frederick, and guarantee the red ink to be original work, not in any way a copy or piracy of Mr. Austin's?"

"Yes," said the witness.

"Is there any instance where you might be wrong that you would like to correct?"

"Certainly not—I am not in the habit of signing things before I have considered them" (a little angrily, alas!).

"Very well; will you look at page 37 where there is an arrangement of 'Seven Sheep Skins' printed in red as the work of Mr. Ketèlbey?"

He did so.

"Now please look at page 47 of Mr. Austin's score of *Polly* and tell me, do you see the same tune there?"

"Yes."

"Do you detect any difference in the tunes?"—a long hot pause. The Judge asked Sir Frederick kindly to take his time and offered him a glass of water.

Eventually Sir Frederick faced Counsel again. "No, except that one is a tone higher than the other."

"But it is in red and you have certified it to be original."

"Yes, I see," said Sir Frederick, now in distress.

"Only one more question," said Luxmoore, "You would not suggest that putting another man's tune up a tone gives you the copyright?"

"No, of course not."

That was the end of the case. The Judge was very severe with the witnesses who allowed a great figure in British music to put his foot in it thus. Columbia had to pay damages and deliver up all the records. Austin was nearly prosecuted for obstruction when they were dumped in the mews where he had his studio; it is queer to think that Columbia and H.M.V. are now as united as a binary star.

Another, more local, adventure in the law court was an altruistic affair. I was off from the studio one day in 1935, in a station taxi, a good old tank of twenty years' service, with intent to catch a tube train in time to conduct the *matinée* of *Henry IV* at His Majesty's Theatre. At a crossing on the Common, my chariot paused, went on, paused again, and finally continued at its top speed of about eight miles an hour. A quarter of a mile away a private car approached at a smart speed, safe enough if my old driver had been more resolute, when the oncomer could have got through behind us, but as it was he hit us four-square abeam and capsized us in a shower of glass. The two drivers had a good shout at one another without taking any notice of me, but, though shaken up, I wasn't much hurt and called up another taxi which got me to the theatre in time for George Robey's big speech.

There was a lawsuit and I gave evidence for the cabby, estimating the speed of our assailant at 30 miles an hour.

Counsel, cross-examining: "How do you arrive at that speed?"

"I know the distance is about a quarter of a mile to the corner," I replied, "and he took about 30 seconds to do it."

Counsel rose to the bait—"and can you, sir, in face of an accident estimate time so exactly in seconds?"

"Would you like to test it?" said I, handing him my stop-watch.

"I most certainly would," said he.

"Very well, when I signal, press the button, and when I signal again, press it again, and give the watch face down to his Lordship."

There was dead silence in court till the watch revealed 30 seconds dead.

"Most remarkable," said the Judge.

"Not at all," said I loftily, "I do it every day in the studio!"

The cabman won and got a new cab; his solicitor thanked me and asked for the secret.

"It is quite simple," I explained, "you hum mentally a quick march—say the British Grenadiers—and 30 bars of it at MM=120 gives you 30 seconds on the watch."

Giving "expert" evidence in the High Court can be good fun and is well remunerated. Neither the Judges nor Counsel know very much about the technical side of music, and though the "expert witnesses" are supposed to be strictly impartial it is very seldom that they are. There was one case in which I used the theory of permutations, long before Mr. Littlewood started to make his fortune out of them. It was a case of plagiarism tried before Mr. Justice Eve, and in this case Frederic Austin was on the other side and had prepared a list of coincidences between two tunes, which, he said, could not be accidental.

Now, Mr. Justice Eve not only did not understand music but disliked it intensely; he once sent a rude message to Mr. Justice Astbury during the "Folly Case" to enquire if it was necessary to turn the High Court into a music hall, and it was obvious that some non-musical logic was necessary to make any impression upon him. I made some enquiries and found to my great surprise that the Judge had published a little book of verse, not bad verse either, and this proved most useful. One of our "expert" musical witnesses was dear kind Julius Harrison, who, being asked in cross-examination to access the odds against two composers having as many as ten coincidences in sixteen bars, replied airily, "About 20 to 1." This caused a lot of laughter on the other side, and their opinion evidently was that the correct betting should be about 50,000 to1.

At the luncheon interval I expressed the wish that I had been asked that question, and our Counsel said, "Very well, I will see to it that it is put to you, if possible, by the other side."

When I entered the box, I started on the job of demolishing Austin's coincidences. One of them was that a pizzicato passage in one tune was illegally imitated by using a harp. I said to the Judge, "Well, there is nothing illegal in having a harp in your orchestra, and, if you do, all you can do is to pluck it—you can't bow it or blow it. If, when plucked, it sounds like a string pizzicato, that is just too bad, you cannot put a hundred harpists permanently out of employment under the Copyright Act of 1911."

This seemed to amuse the Judge, who thought that was quite a pity. He said, "You heard Mr. Harrison say that the odds were 20 to 1 against two men writing a tune with all these ten things in both. Do you agree with him?"

I replied, "Not quite."

Counsel for the other side: "20 to 1, I should think not, 20,000 to 1 more likely."

The Judge raised a restraining hand. "At what figure," he said, "would you put the odds yourself, Mr. Irving?"

"At about 19 to 1," I said, after a little consideration.

That caused what might be described as a slight sensation and I was invited to prove that in a class of twenty, set to write a tune of this kind, one of the twenty would actually write the "pirated melody" note for note with all Austin's ten coincidences.

Another of Austin's coincidences was that the last three notes of each of the strains were two short and one long accentuated, and this is where my little bit of prosodical research came in useful.

"This alleged coincidence," I said, "is merely a common place. It is known as an anapaest and occurs in thousands of pieces of music of this kind."

Counsel repeated the Greek term and said, "Well, I hope this means something to His Lordship, but it means nothing to me."

"I think it may," said I, artfully.

Then counsel really put his foot in it. "Of course," he said "you have come prepared with some of these thousands of instances—these musical anapaests?

"No," I said, "but you have under your elbow a pile of music, would you kindly lend me the top copy?"

He passed it over. It was, as I had observed, the "Merry Widow Waltz".

"Without bursting into song, which I am sure would displease your Lordship," I continued, "it is a matter of optical observation that the tune goes Lah-di-dah-di- Lah-di-da-di, pom, pom, POM. That pom, pom, Pom, is the anapaest to which I refer and one of Austin's ten coincidences."

"To use an anapaest is certainly not a breach of copyright," said the Judge, and I felt considerable fraternal satisfaction in avenging Harrison by hoisting counsel with his own petard.

But the removal from the pile of *The Merry Widow* also disclosed another popular waltz, that from *The Maid of the Mountains* by my old friend Harold Fraser Simson, easily recognisable by the picture of José Collins upon the cover. I borrowed this from the very surprised barrister and offered the two copies to the Judge.

"If I could persuade your Lordship to risk a glance at these copies, I think you would find something very informative about musical plagiarism," I said.

"Certainly not," said the Judge, "I know nothing about music, that is what you are here for."

"This has nothing to do with music, my Lord, it is only an optical observation."

"Very well," said the Judge reluctantly, and peered at the two refrains.

"If you will look at the first two bars of *The Merry Widow*, my Lord, you will see there are four notes which I described as Lah-di-da di."

He said, "Yes, I see them."

"In the third and fourth bar," I continued, "the same four notes are repeated Lah-di-dah-di."

Everybody was now highly enjoying the proceedings.

"If you will now kindly refer to *The Maid of the Mountains*," I continued, "you will find the same four notes, only instead of Lah-di-dah-di being repeated, they are set out with each note repeated La-lah, Da-di, Da-da, Di-di. The same coincidence occurs in the bars numbered 5 to 8."

The Judge agreed.

"Very well, here is a man who takes another man's tune, places each note twice and makes a fortune out of the result without anybody complaining about a breach of copyright or anything else."

Counsel: "But we are not trying a case about *The Maid of the Mountains* or *The Merry Widow*."

"No," I replied, "all these waltzes are very much alike and it is ridiculous to complain of a breach of copyright just because you both use a common lyrical form."

So, after fifteen minutes' exposition of permutations, I sat down, having proved conclusively that, in a class of twenty, one student would duplicate the original tune. Counsel shrugged his shoulders and did not cross-examine any further; there he made a mistake, as, in giving judgment, Mr. Justice Eve said that no attempt had been made to disprove my figures and he must accept them as correct.

The end of my musico-legal career was, owing to my cockiness of which I have complained before, a complete washout.

Frederic Austin was again in it, acting through the Performing Right Society. A Canadian impresario had staged *The Beggar's Opera*, and, not being willing to pay Austin's royalty, had engaged a local composer of ability and reputation to make a new score on the old tunes which Gay had used. Austin complained that he had been pirated; the other composer swore he had not so much as seen Austin's score. It was referred to arbitration and I was appointed by the High Court as an Assessor to "try and determine" the suit; the Assessor for the other side was my old friend Hubert Foss of the Oxford University Press, and we met as enjoined by Statute to select a barrister to sit with us to advise on questions of law.

We dined—it was in the days of sirloins—at the Falstaff in Fleet Street, and over a Cordial Médoc discussed the probabilities.

"My chap is a fine musician and wouldn't steal anything," said Hubert.

"I know that," I said, "but he has protested too much. You must have noticed that Austin when he added anything original to Gay's score put his initials against the join?"

"Yes," said Foss, "what of it?"

"Well," said I, "your man has done the same but yet he has sworn that he has never *seen* Austin's score!"

Foss reported the vulnerable point, his clients withdrew and paid up. I lost my chance of actually sitting as a "justice in fair round belly with good capon lined", not to mention the considerable fees that would have accrued.

The author at work

In the studio with Dr. Vaughan Williams

CHAPTER XXXII

Music in Films

★

EVERYBODY NOWADAYS thinks he can write incidental music. I had hundreds of letters when I was music director at Ealing Studios offering to do it and dozens enquiring how to do it. Many correspondents wished to take up a career to "write music for films" and had to be informed that film music was just the same as any other music except that it was paid for at a higher rate. There is one advantage in writing film music; millions of people have to listen to it whether they like it or not. I would not say that the managers of cinemas are remarkable for their good taste, and if the music in their current film has achieved success or notoriety they are inclined to turn on the "juice" and let the public have it *fff*. In the old silent films the music was necessary not only to illustrate the action but to cover the noise of the camera and the chocolate crunching. It was fitted to the film with varying degrees of appropriateness, depending on the playing of the local orchestra for its effectiveness and providing employment for hundreds of players.

The music director received with the film a list of music suggested for it, and all kinds of music were roped in for the task, classical, light and vulgar, particularly the last. The opening of the Schubert "Unfinished" Symphony was in the catalogue as a light, flowing agitato, and the Beethoven *Coriolanus* Overture was recommended for hewing down trees. Any number of people made their first acquaintance with the classics by being compelled to listen to them in this way.

The conductor was expected to mark any important happenings, especially comic ones, with a suitable noise; a donkey brayed on the trombone and a custard pie arrived to the ping of a tom-tom. The music never ceased; when the large band went to eat, a small band took its place, and when they were both tired out, up popped the organ to carry on.

The arrival of the talking film revolutionised all this, and, sad to say, rendered the live orchestras redundant. Music could be recorded with large symphony orchestras and played just as well in Littleborough as in Leicester Square. Special music could be written for each film and fitted with great accuracy, the synchronisation being, of course, made automatic by the fact that the picture and the sound were carried upon the same film. The composition of the music provided a lucrative occupation and the composer frequently made as much out of one film as Mozart got for all his operas put together. One of the tasks I set myself in Ealing was to see that this Tom Tiddler's ground was populated by the right people, and that composers of good music should be able, if they wished, by spending three months on film music to write what they liked, however uncommercial, during the other nine.

Now music to sound films is quite a different affair to the setting needed for the silent variety. It does not have to act as a substitute for dialogue, but, on the contrary, has to be kept down to a low level so that the words can be heard. What it can do, however, is to indicate the thoughts and emotions of the players and the essence of their emotional surroundings, and that is where the good composer comes in. Vaughan Williams, for instance, wrote some main title music for *Scott of the Antarctic* which, transferred to a scene for climbing the glacier, fitted as exactly as if it had been composed specially for that sequence, and I have known many instances in which the music written for one part of a film could be transferred to another because there was an intrinsic quality which belonged to the film as a whole.

Dr. Vaughan Williams has an idea that the film should be shot to the accompaniment of the music, but here I think he is over-valuing the composer's work. Millions of people who go to films know nothing about music at all, and there are quite a number of film fans who positively dislike music. I think a good composer is just as likely to write good dramatic music for a film as a bad one, and that it is right and proper that he should have the benefit of the good fees paid for this work; but his art must not be allowed to be a stumbling block or to prevent the enjoyment of the pictorial side by people who are not in sympathy with him. That implies that the music must always be subsidiary and ancillary and cannot be allowed to develop on formal lines for musical reasons only; it is not being played at a concert, its principal effect should be upon the subconscious mind, and if the film is a good film the music will be felt rather than listened to.

All this seems pretty obvious, but an astonishing number of people have the queerest views upon music, and at lectures I have given I have been asked by intelligent people questions which indicate a microscopical amount of musical culture.

After the film score has been composed, cut, and fitted there are two important requisites. First, the conductor must know exactly what he is going to do, what effects he wants, exactly where they come, and how to get them out of the score; he must time everything to one-third of a second and make certain that the composer and the director are in reasonable agreement, then he must vet the score to see that it includes the colouring and emphasis that the action demands and provide for the sometimes unreasonable cuts and alterations which may be made to a supposedly final version of the film. He should employ the very best orchestra procurable, not single players put together for the occasion but an experienced body of *confréres* who are used to playing together and who know a good conductor when they see one.

I can best describe what follows by quoting a few paragraphs from a paper which I read to the Royal Musical Association, with Frank Howes in the chair, on March 9, 1950:—

"Eventually all is completed and an orchestra of fifty to eighty players is engaged and assembled in the recording theatre. The players sit in tiers, as at a symphony concert, though the groups are more widely separated; bright banks of light illumine the scene; there are four or five microphones on booms, stands and slings. At the back is a celluloid screen on to which the picture will be projected when called for by the conductor, moving at the immutable rate of 90 feet per minute. The conductor will rehearse the music with the composer at hand to make corrections, suggestions, additions and cuts; and a musical assistant will be listening in the recording booth to the sound as it comes over the monitor from the floor. This sound differs from that heard by the conductor and is a truer index of what will go on the film.

"When all has been tonally adjusted the composer and conductor will go into the booth, and the musical assistant will mount the rostrum, a procedure which generally leads to more adjustments of microphones and positions by the recording and sound engineer. At some of the rehearsals the picture will be run, the music each time being brought a little nearer to synchronisation, and if any instrumentalist is concerned in a special effect, it is explained to him, and he is shown the 'mute' if necessary. The final rehearsal is recorded upon a glass disc and played back to all concerned. The musicians hear their work, any necessary corrections are made and a 'take' is announced.

"Now vanishes anything in the nature of experiment or improvisation, everyone is taut, concentrated and careful. This is where the value of a first-rate orchestra is shown; like a famous regiment going into action, it combines dash with experience, and confidence with caution. Mistakes are sometimes made; the conductor gets out of time with the picture, or, following it too closely, gives an undecided or faulty beat; a player misses an entry, plays a wrong note, or 'breaks' a right one. Such mistakes are never regarded as blameworthy, the conductor simply says 'cut', and when the 'mute' has been rewound, the shot is started again. It may have to be restarted five or six times; there are so many to be satisfied, the composer and conductor as to the music, the director as to the effects, the recordist as to the modulation of his 'track' and the balance of the various microphones employed. When one is right another may be wrong, but patience is the order of the day and sooner or later a 'take' is obtained which satisfies all concerned.

"All is not yet over. A 'cover take' has to be made in case anything should happen to the negative in its passage through the laboratory. And so the day proceeds, 90 minutes recording, 10 minutes for coffee, 70 minutes more and then an hour for lunch. If things do not go smoothly—and there are many annoying things that may happen to film, sound-camera, microphones, amplifiers, and projection machines which have nothing to do with technicians or players—time may press hardly at the end of the afternoon and completion of the day's schedule may be in doubt. That is another occasion when the tried warrior is worth his weight in gold; speed without hurry, tension without excitement, mutual confidence, and, above all, unflagging concentration have been known to work miracles against the clock. Next morning the protagonists hear their work when the 'prints' come in from the laboratory; comment is quite free and no criticism is resented, but it is seldom nowadays that anything has to be re-made, as manipulative surgery serves to correct errors of incidence and timing; gross mistakes of balance may be rectified mechanically by re-recording from the track; and small musical flaws, however annoying, are seldom of sufficient importance to call for drastic measures."

The Philharmonia Orchestra was more than half my battle, and if there was trouble or delay at recording sessions, it was nearly always the fault of the composer, the director, the editor, the copyist, or me. One should never forget that for a man to put a piece of brass or wood to his mouth and produce sounds of the pitch, quality and style expected by the conductor is a miracle, and not to be taken for granted because it occurs a thousand times a day.

CHAPTER XXXIII

Criticism and the Critics

★

THIS CHAPTER VERY nearly got itself omitted; but at my age I think one may take a risk. Fifty years ago Press notices were highly valued by "the tyro". *The Stage* and *The Era* were purchased regularly for twopence and sixpence respectively and scanned for the notices, which very seldom did anything except mildly praise. In the larger towns, which had their own newspapers, the notices were occasionally critical; the *Manchester Guardian* in particular was inclined to drop a heavy hand upon poor shows. In London, of course, it was quite different.

I have offered the opinion elsewhere that the most difficult job in the film studio is that of the man who has to sell the film. In the musical world most certainly the most difficult job is that of the critic who has to express an opinion of an explanatory kind more often than not without seeing the score or having any opportunity for finding out the composer's intentions or method.

Just to listen to a piece of music is not at all sufficient for forming a considered opinion upon its merit; music gets daily more and more complicated and involves sound-texture and rhythm-nuance which demand more than one or two hearings. In slating something he does not like, the critic must be sure that he is not missing some merit; in praising what he enjoys he must be sure that the music is original and genuine. He has to go day after day and week after week to listen to works of which, however good, he is bound sooner or later to get a little tired.

In addition to this, what he writes must be readable as well as informative, and critics can be forgiven if sometimes they devote their attention to little things that do not matter very much. I remember one notice which did not mention a very good orchestral performance on a first night except to say that we played the National Anthem in A Flat, but I must admit that its author was a reporter rather than a critic.

So in order to avoid any misunderstanding I will disinfect this chapter with a moral, which is, "It is better to be slated than ignored." Critics very seldom bother about flaying a bad artist but take the trouble to discuss one whose performance is disliked for reasons other than incompetence. I used to think that everyone I met had read my Press notices, good or bad, and get very hot under the skin when someone disagreed or overlooked, but the really mortifying disappointment was when one was left out altogether and all the hard work of preparation and rehearsal had gone for nothing.

Some of our critics, to my knowledge, have been most helpful to young composers. I went down with William Walton to consult Ernest Newman about the opera which Walton was contemplating. We found the old man in his garden studio superintending the filling up of his private air-raid shelter which was dug down under the front door. I advised him rather impertinently to dig deeper rather than destroy. His advice to William was full of wisdom, and the little room was filled with an encyclopaedic aura which very nearly materialised Richard Wagner.

Sydney Carroll was once a critic, but after a small disagreement about a well-known actress, he gave up criticism for management; whether he preferred it I do not know, but I am sure that, unlike the Duke of Plaza Toro, he found it more exciting. I have received many kindnesses from critics which have been pleasant and profitable, and though I have had my share of "wiggings" I should be ungrateful if I did not acknowledge the balance on the credit side.

Of course, they make mistakes sometimes. There is a famous story about an eminent and talented critic who disliked the playing of the French pianist Cortot. Cortot was to play the Schumann concerto on Wednesday with the Phil and the "Emperor" on Friday with the B.B.C.; the critic wrote two bad notices in advance and went away for a holiday. His paper printed Friday's notice on Thursday and Cortot was approached with a view to appeasement. "It is all right," said he, "it will be a lovely story to tell in Paris."

It is difficult, however, to bear adverse criticism patiently when it is uninformed or ignorant; the two notices that have annoyed me most were both by ladies. I have already mentioned them. The first was upon my score of *Comus*, which was taken out of Handel's music, and, probably remembering the film I did about Handel's life, *The Great Mr. Handel*, referred to the "lush" harmonies I had introduced. Now this was very hard, since all Handel's scores were checked up at the British Museum and there was not a single note that was not either to be found in the original or justified by Handel's figured bass.

The other lady scarified my arrangement of Dlibes' *Coppélia* for the International Ballet. "I altered the original score", she said. The first reason was that there isn't one, and the second that if a score produced with ninety players is to be played by twenty-five, something has got to be done about the band parts. I offered to discuss with this lady any points in the orchestration with which she disagreed and received the astonishing reply that she knew nothing about orchestration but did not see why that precluded her from criticising it. So I gave it up.

I will conclude this chapter with a little story about my friend, Philip Page, the music and dramatic critic, whose praise of the music did much to further the success of the original production of *The Two Bouquets*. Page and I agreed on the two main points, (a) that I am a good musician, (b) that he is a good critic, but on many other matters we could, and did, have hearty and healthy difference.

Page in his youth had also been in the choir, and we were discussing the hymns we disliked most. Among them were Dykes' best-sellers and Cowper's blood fountains; while we laughed a little at Neale's gold, milk and honey, and at the prowling Midianites—Neale again. But we were in full and glorious agreement about the best of them all. We differed over the tune; he liked old Dowland's strong minor, whereas I prefer Dr. Croft's gloat in A Major. But what magnificent words! Here is a flag to wave for a man with any sort of a Creed. Grant sees a God who is indeed Omnipotent, Omniscient and Omnipresent. It always warmed my heart to sing these great words, and though I expect they will be familiar to my readers, I am going to print them in full, all six verses.

O worship the King, all glorious above;
O gratefully sing His power and His love:
Our Shield and Defender, the Ancient of Days,
Pavilioned in splendour, and girded with praise.

O tell of His might, O sing of His grace,
Whose robe is the light, whose canopy space;
His chariots of wrath the deep thunder-clouds form,
And dark is His path on the wings of the storm.

The earth with its store of wonders untold,
Almighty! Thy power hath founded of old,
Hath stablished it fast by a changeless decree,
And round it hath cast, like a mantle, the sea.

Thy bountiful care what tongue can recite?
It breathes in the air, it shines in the light,
It streams from the hills, it descends to the plain,
And sweetly distils in the dew and the rain.

Frail children of dust, and feeble as frail,
In Thee do we trust, nor find Thee to fail;
Thy mercies how tender, how firm to the end,
Our Maker, Defender, Redeemer, and Friend!

O measureless Might! ineffable Love!
While angels delight to hymn Thee above,
Thy ransomed creation, though feeble their lays,
With true adoration shall ring to Thy praise.

I once did a little music criticism myself, starting as a deputy, but I do not think this was wise, as however strong may be one's determination to be impartial, a fighter in the arena is bound to have more fixed ideas than a critic in the stalls. Music of the moment, with the twelve-tone scale and what-not, is a highly complicated affair and it is quite easy for the mountebank to cover vacuousness with strange noises and dislocated counterpoint; on the other hand, in exposing this one may be injuring a budding Stravinsky or Scriabin. As just a concertgoer, I may be allowed to say that I do not like the second part of the Beethoven Choral Symphony, but as a critic I should not dare to start with the view that Beethoven could write anything mediocre. So I am very glad to be a composer, however second-rate, and make something, preferring it very much to the duty of continually talking about somebody else's music. And in writing music for films I had the consolation of knowing that, whether my music was good or bad, millions of people had to listen to it whether they liked it or not.

CHAPTER XXXIV

Rawsthorne, Walton and Vaughan Williams

★

THREE COMPOSERS have honoured me greatly by dedicating to me a serious major work; Alan Rawsthorne and William Walton string quartets, and Ralph Vaughan Williams his Sonfonia Antartica.

Alan Rawsthorne, whose Second Symphony was commissioned by the Royal Philharmonic Society, cannot any longer be classed with our "promising" composers; he has carved for himself a place in the front rank. He has a robust and very individual style of his own, solidly contrapuntal, set out on an orchestral palette with great variety of colouring, sometimes vivid and violent and sometimes delicate and opaline. It is perhaps a little impertinent of me to enter into a description of his talent; in ten years time it will be unnecessary. Rawsthorne has a keen sense of humour and a pretty wit, characteristics not so common among musicians as one could wish; like the other two subjects of this chapter I have found him humble and single-minded in the face of his art. The quartet is not very often played, but it will be.

Sir William Walton is, of course, one of the few great composers who have written any humorous music, and his collaboration with Miss Sitwell in *Façade* is perhaps better known to the ordinary public than his great works. Walton is very modest and unostentatious; he works very slowly and carefully, asking and acting upon the advice of his musical friends when in any doubt. I had the great pleasure of working in the recording booth at the making of *Belshazzar's Feast*. Here were gathered under Walton's baton the Huddersfield Choir, the Liverpool Philharmonic Orchestra, two Brass Bands and Dennis Noble; I am quite sure that never has such a tremendous volume of sound been emitted from a recorded disc. This necessitated an intimate knowledge of the score, and a swift and sensitive balance of the tone values in the booth, so that the details were clearly shown without any obstruction of the main themes.

That was a very difficult job but fascinating; it could not in its nature be perfect, but then, perfection was hardly required. In the middle of it that fine singer, Dennis Noble. pitched upon an A flat solo, which I thought slightly sharp. It was a quarter to one upon a fine Sunday morning and the singers and players responded to my request for another "take" without enthusiasm. I insisted and they repeated the section, but I still was not satisfied. My protest this time was received with a groan of execration and we all went off to lunch.

It is a very remarkable record, and when the finished disc was played over by H.M.V., I enquired about the note of disputed pitch. Tested by a tuning fork, it was a quarter of a tone sharp, and it is a good thing that it did not matter because there was now nothing one could do about it; Walton could not even have altered the score because it was half-way between one note and the next; so there it stands, a very tiny flaw in a splendid performance.

The Quartet which is dedicated to me has a lovely slow movement, somewhat unfashionable in these days of atonalism and twelve-tone scales, that will remind many of Brahms and Elgar. At the first performance by the Blech Quartet at the B.B.C. Hall I sat beside the lovely lady who I think inspired it, and it now always sounds to me like an elegy. I have been told by my enemies that the last movement represents me, quarrelsome, disputatious, didactic and violent; but as I do not admit any of these adjectives, I take a more good-humoured view of the music.

Sir William's Te Deum for the Coronation Service will have taken many people back to the Golden Age of English music, though I think I caught a glance of "Mene, Mene" on the way. His opera *Troilus and Cressida* has a libretto based by Christopher Hassall upon Chaucer's poem and not upon Shakespeare's play. It is a very fine work, equal I think to anything produced during my lifetime.

I first met Ralph Vaughan Williams in my early days with the Phil; he and Norman O'Neill were great friends. He once wrote a piece for solo violin—I always thought it should have been solo flute—called *The Lark Ascending*, and it was to have been played at a Phil concert by a distinguished if bad-mannered foreign lady violinist. When she turned up to rehearsal she knew nothing about the work, and swore that she had not received the score which I sent to her. The fact that I had her signature on the registration receipt did not help us, neither did the lady's offer to read the music at the concert, as it was a rhapsodic composition and the lark's tail soared hundreds of feet above the music stand. V.W. was furious; he stamped off in a temper and I got a completely wrong impression of the man. Closer contact in recent years has shown a great artist—an inspired musician, a humble follower of his art, always ready to learn and seeking to be informed, generous and altruistic, continually planning to help other musicians less fortunately placed than himself. The music critic of a daily paper once accused him of "swank"; those who knew V.W. were furious; if ever this scurrilous term was ineptly and falsely applied, it was here, and it would be quite easy to refute it completely, chapter and verse.

I think it was Muir Mathieson who first lured the old Maestro into films. He composed a score for *49th Parallel*, and I did not think it was very good or the subject very well suited to his individual traits of composition. I got him to Ealing for *The Loves of Joanna Godden*, a rustic romance for which he wrote some grand music for sheep, cows, and the farmers. It called upon him to describe, for the first time in his life, foot-and-mouth disease, which he did with such fidelity that one could almost smell the burning carcasses. The music had a gentle climactic melody at the finish which might have made the film, but was choked down in recording to accommodate some fatuous dialogue.

Some of the "sheep" music I was able to use again in a film entitled *Bitter Springs*, set in Australia; after all, sheep are sheep, and a little change in orchestral colouring will soon flip them over to the Antipodes.

In this film there was a sequence where a baby kangaroo performed a sort of little ballet, finishing up by leaping into its mother's pouch, and I had set this to a little rhythmic flute tune beautifully played by Gareth Morris. One of our most distinguished critics, reviewing the film upon the radio, praised this highly, saying that nobody but Vaughan Williams could have composed it. Almost before the lady finished speaking, V.W. had dashed off a letter to the *Radio Times* to say that on the contrary it was the composition of his collaborator, Mr. Ernest Irving. (V.W's good will is better than his calligraphy, and they printed Mr. as Dr.; in spite of the published disclaimer, this "honorary" degree has stuck to me ever since). Not only did he insist that I share the credit but he also wanted to give me half his fee; it was with great difficulty that I parried this by suggesting a joint donation to the musical charities.

When Ealing Studios decided to make *Scott of the Antarctic*, everybody agreed that, if Dr. Vaughan Williams could be interested, he was the one man in the world to write the score. I rang him up; he liked the idea, but in view of his experiences with *Joanna* began to lay down conditions. "Don't tell me," I said, "come and tell the directors"; and we had a big round-table conference at which he told us all his plans which were agreed enthusiastically and unanimously.

About a fortnight afterwards, I asked the Editorial Department to get out a rough list of the timings of sequences where music would be required, explaining that Dr. Vaughan Williams was not a regular professional composer of film music and that it might take some time to get his score fitted to the action. The list was sent to Vaughan Williams, but by return I received a holograph letter, about as legible as the Rosetta stone, thanking me for the timings which he said were a little late to be of use. He had that morning posted to me the full score of the whole work, including a pianoforte sketch for use at rehearsals!

He must have had some of the themes in his mind beforehand, of course, and not all of the music went into the film, but it was all so akin to the thoughts and emotions that stirred that devoted little party of explorers that I was often able to move it about inside the film, applying some of it to incidents for which it was not designed. For instance, the music composed for the main titles—or overture—to the film, exactly fitted the climbing of the Glacier and stopped with a shuddering roll on the bass drum as the party reached the very edge of a fathomless crevasse—one more crotchet would have swallowed up the whole expedition!

Such music, by such a master, was not to be allowed to die with the film, and Dr. Vaughan Williams based upon it his Sinfonia Antartica which was first performed by the Hallé Orchestra under Sir John Barbirolli, in Manchester, and then in London at a Royal Philharmonic Society's concert. He dedicated it to me and gave me the manuscript score. I, in turn, presented the score to the Society, and it now lies in their collection at the British Museum, side by side with the manuscript of Beethoven's "Choral Symphony". I should call it a symphonic poem rather than a symphony; it is written for a huge orchestra with choir and solo-voice; there was a good deal of fuss made about the introduction of the "wind machine"—a small matter, and no solecism.

The Sinfornia Antartica presents an outstanding example of film music upon the concert platform, and I think it will be played, or at any rate part of it, when many classically designed works have disappeared.

My association with this great-minded man has been one of the pleasantest things in my musical life, and, as with Walton, I think it is a great privilege to have been of some assistance to him in his work.

CHAPTER XXXV

The Royal Philharmonic Society

★

NORMAN O'NEILL appears earlier in this book as the talented composer of theatre music and a very popular member of the Savage Club. His real interest in life, however, was not in these things but in serious music. He was the treasurer and mainspring of the Royal Philharmonic Society which he was instrumental in steering through the many vissitudes of the First World War, a difficult time indeed for such institutions. The machinery of the old Society was becoming rusty and the orchestra contained too many old professors whose fingers were no longer as nimble as their wits. Deputies at rehearsals and concerts were far too many among the professionals, and some new blood was obviously needed.

Many years ago a well-known conductor said to me "There are three principles to be followed in forming an orchestra. (1) Get the best musicians. (2) Get the best musicians. (3) When you have got the best musicians, sack the worst of them and get some better ones."

This was the principle that Norman proposed to adopt, but you cannot engage the best players until you know who they are, and the best way to find that out is to have them play with you, or under you in small combinations, such as theatre orchestras. With this in view, Norman got me elected about forty years ago, first an Associate and then a Member, and finally proposed me for the Committee—then called Directors.

There was a ballot in which I tied for last place with an old member. Sir Alexander Mackenzie was the Chairman and we were paraded at his left hand to hear the result. I started to make a speech offering to retire in favour of the proved warrior, and received from Sir Alexander's pointed toe-cap a savage kick upon an old football lesion which absolutely paralysed me. Asked to wait outside, I limped off the scene and begged from the steward some hot water to lave my injured fibula.

On my return to the room, Sir Alexander said that I had been unanimously elected to the Committee, as Mr. O'Neill had a definite task for me in the reconstruction of the Society's orchestra. That launched me upon a mission in partnership with Norman, and the scar, which still gives me twinges on rainy days, remains to remind me of Sir Alexander and his powerful spur to smite.

In those days it was impossible for orchestral concert players to make a living out of symphonic work, they had to fill in with theatrical engagements; so we turned out attention to finding such jobs for the players we wanted, where they would be permitted to send deputies and attend our concerts. To manoeuvre this, without damage to the theatre performance, was a delicate and difficult task and entailed careful planning to see that the theatre deputies were well rehearsed; on one occasion at the Piccadilly Theatre I had thirty-three deputies out of thirty-four players! My boss listened to the first act with trepidation, but at the end admitted that the performance was first class. "Why can't we have those fellows all the time?" he asked.

We also started a very useful schedule of orchestral concerts, so that the Queen's Hall Orchestra, the London Symphony Orchestra, and the Albert Hall Orchestra all chose different dates, none of which clashed with ours. The improvement in the orchestral playing was magical, and our synthetic orchestra gave London the best music it had heard for years. Then two things happened to the Phil, which changed everything again—the B.B.C. and Sir Thomas Beecham.

As everyone knows, the Kaiser War sent up taxes and salaries to such an extent that it became impossible to give high-class symphony concerts without heavy loss, even if all the seats were sold. What was perhaps even more important was that the cost of rehearsals increased to such a point that new and difficult modern works could not be thoroughly prepared except at prohibitive cost. The B.B.C., with its large income from licences, was better equipped to cope with the new conditions, and at the time it looked as if the old Society would be swallowed up. Negotiations took place between the Society, Sir Thomas Beecham and Sir John Reith, then head of the B.B.C., which must, I suppose, be regarded even now as semi-confidential; perhaps I may be allowed to say that the Royal Philharmonic Society very nearly got control of broadcast music, and that I think it a very good thing both for music and the Society that they did not. However, a working agreement was made which avoided the obliteration of the Phil, ensuring its independence while giving it a certain amount of support.

The B.B.C. Symphony Orchestra was organised under Dr. Boult, emerging competitively as a concert-giving body, and Sir Thomas started to create (in conjunction with the Society) the London Philharmonic Orchestra. All kinds of plans for any number of concerts were made, the orchestra was expanded and improved under the principles laid down earlier in this chapter, and for a time all was roseate and up-springing. Public competition from the B.B.C. Symphony Orchestra was counteracted by an enormous new audience of concert-goers created by the B.B.C. broadcasts of symphonic music; even Beethoven, for all his foreign birth, was roped in as a victory symbol and millions of people were brought to realise the charms of Mozart, Brahms, Debussy and Ravel, who twenty years earlier would not have gone within a mile of them.

Then, alas, the Second World War disorganised everything. Luckily, however, the government had observed the salutary effect of good music in war-time, and C.E.M.A. was formed to support music and the other arts, under conditions in which they would have been quite unable to support themselves. Thus the old Society was again saved for its Members, Associates and Fellows, who still came up in full numbers with their subscriptions, donations and guarantees. Keith Douglas, the honorary secretary, who died while in its service, left £10,000 to the foundation fund. Ritson Smith, who succeeded him, and luckily for the Society suffered from insomnia, put in one hundred and twenty hours a week on its business. All through the years there have been found busy professional musical men—and amateurs too—to give their time and energy to the running of this honourable and valuable institution. I have not the least doubt that it will be in full activity a hundred years hence.

At the end of the Second World War, for reasons which need not be discussed in this book. Sir Thomas Beecham formed a new orchestra, the "Royal Philharmonic", upon the lines laid down earlier in this chapter. The Delius Trust helped its inauguration by giving a Delius Festival and it is now to be heard at nearly all the Society's concerts, where its admirers claim that it has set a new standard in British orchestral playing. As I write, it is preparing to open its new season with a Brahms programme, in which, if we are lucky, we may hear a repetition of that magical performance of the Third Symphony given by Sir Thomas three years ago.

All through this book I have endeavoured to avoid any kind of braggadocio, indeed there has been very little to brag about, but there are three thing that I am very proud of and I propose to set them down here.

First, the honorary degree of the Royal Academy of Music conferred upon me in 1945 upon the proposal of Theodore Holland.

Second, the dedications of Alan Rawsthorne's String Quartet, William Walton's String Quartet, and Vaughan William's Sinfonia Antartica.

Third, the honorary membership of the Royal Philharmonic

Society conferred in 1951. Past honorary members, of whom there are sixty-four, include Mendelssohn, Auber, Hummel, Meyerbeer, Rossini, Berlioz, Gade, Halévy, Liszt, Anton Rubinstein, Wagner, Gounod, Heller, Brahms, Raff, Randegger, Verdi, Dvôrák, Sarasate, Bottesini, von Bülow, Moszkowski, Saint-Saëns, Clara Schumann, Svendsen, Grieg, Tchaikowsky, Ysaye, Paderewski, Bruch, Glazounov, Rachmaninoff, Massenet, Richter, Richard Strauss, Kubelik, Nikisch, Ravel and Frederic Austin.

The present honorary members are:— Cortot, Strawinsky, Toscanini, Stokowski, Sibelius, Casals and, quite unbelievably, myself.

What I am doing in such a gallery heaven only knows, but I am the only surviving British honorary member. Though unable, through illness, to attend the committee meetings, I still keep in close touch with the honorary secretary and do all I can in the way of advice and support. Humbly equipped as I am for the service of great music, I have derived great pleasure and satisfaction in the work I have been able to do through the old Society, and I beg of any young musician, devoted to good music, who may chance to read this chapter, if not a member, to write to the Honorary Secretary at 4 St. James's Square, London, S.W.1, and I know he will be delighted to give him every information about the Society's aims and activities.

EPILOGUE

By Derek Hudson

These are the last words of his book that Irving lived to write, and the emphasis on the "Phil" is one that he would have approved. His death came as a great shock to someone, like myself, who had received his keen and lively letters almost to the end; more of a shock perhaps than it was to those who saw with their own eyes how much stronger he was in mind than in body.

He had planned to write a final chapter called "A Hive of Bees", and had jotted down a characteristic bit of philosophy for an Epilogue:— "You are sure to get the sack sometime; be certain to turn it to your advantage." This he certainly contrived in his own life.

I cannot attempt to construct his final chapter, but his secretary asked him what was going into it, and he replied "A lot of nonsense." She had always imagined, though, that he intended to describe himself working from his bed with all his staff buzzing in and out of his bedroom. He had worked thus for quite eighteen months before his retirement, getting up only on occasions, either to conduct a "session" or to go into the studio to hear the "tracks". There was a notice on his door which read "Danger: Man at Work", and when this got destroyed a second one went up: "Danger: Man STILL at Work".

He was still at work when he died. Music meant everything to him, and I think that in conclusion he might have liked to say so. He was modest about his own success, and very humble in the face of great music, but with it all had the pride of the true craftsman. I think he would have understood the spirit in which I place these lines of Browning's at the end of his book:

"But God has a few of us whom he whispers in the ear;
The rest may reason and welcome; 'tis we musicians know".

GENERAL INDEX

INDEX OF PERSONS

Index of Persons

INDEX OF PLAYS, OPERAS, ETC.

Index of Plays, Operas, Etc.